Furth

"A useful roadmap for developing a more ethical culture, *The Right Thing* is a must-read for anyone from the business school to the board room."

David Cox, SVP and CFO, Economist Group, Americas

"I strongly recommend this book to anyone who thinks ethics matters in business. And for those who don't yet think so, beware; the evidence is growing that people prefer to work for and do business with ethical companies."

Paul Moore, HBOS Whistleblower and Senior Partner at Moore, Carter & Associates

"In these times understanding ethics has never been more important. *The Right Thing* explores the practical realities of ethical behavior; its driving forces and implications."

John Harris, former CEO, Calor

"A hearts and minds, root and branch perspective on ethical business."

Katie Alcott, Founder, Frank Water

"If good leadership is the life blood of a successful organization, then great ethics is the heart beat. *The Right Thing* is a simple to read, approachable framework for the time poor, intelligent business leader to engage with the critical, ethical and moral questions and challenges of business."

Daniel Snell, Founder, Arrival Education

"If long-term success is your business goal, you can't afford not to do the right thing. Sally Bibb provides a fresh look at business ethics and what you can do to instil them in your organization's culture."

Daniel H. Pink, author of *A Whole New Mind* and *Drive*

THE RIGHT THING

THE RIGHT THING

An everyday guide to ethics in business

SALLY BIBB

A John Wiley & Sons, Ltd., Publication

This edition first published 2010
© 2010 John Wiley & Sons Ltd.

Registered office
John Wiley & Sons Ltd, The Atrium, Southern Gate, Chichester, West Sussex, PO19 8SQ, United Kingdom

For details of our global editorial offices, for customer services and for information about how to apply for permission to reuse the copyright material in this book please see our website at www.wiley.com

The right of the author to be identified as the author of this work has been asserted in accordance with the Copyright, Designs and Patents Act 1988.

All rights reserved. No part of this publication may be reproduced, stored in a retrieval system, or transmitted, in any form or by any means, electronic, mechanical, photocopying, recording or otherwise, except as permitted by the UK Copyright, Designs and Patents Act 1988, without the prior permission of the publisher.

Wiley also publishes its books in a variety of electronic formats. Some content that appears in print may not be available in electronic books.

Designations used by companies to distinguish their products are often claimed as trademarks. All brand names and product names used in this book are trade names, service marks, trademarks or registered trademarks of their respective owners. The publisher is not associated with any product or vendor mentioned in this book. This publication is designed to provide accurate and authoritative information in regard to the subject matter covered. It is sold on the understanding that the publisher is not engaged in rendering professional services. If professional advice or other expert assistance is required, the services of a competent professional should be sought.

ISBN 978-0-470-68853-3 (paperback), ISBN 978-0-470-97593-0 (ebk),
ISBN 978-0-470-97527-5 (ebk), ISBN 978-0-470-97528-2 (ebk)

A catalogue record for this book is available from the British Library.

Set in 11.5/17pt Jenson Pro by Toppan Best-set Premedia Limited
Printed in Great Britain by TJ International Ltd, Padstow, Cornwall, UK

CONTENTS

ACKNOWLEDGEMENTS

B ook writing is never an individual quest. Writing this one
certainly wasn't and there are a good number of people who
contributed either directly or indirectly and who I would like to
thank.

First and foremost are those from whom, over many years,
the inspiration came to write about ethics. They are the people
who have played a particularly strong part in fuelling my interest
in and thinking on the subject of ethics: my parents, my grand-
father, my friend Jon Cassell, my friend and mentor the late
Gerard Fairtlough, my occasional mentor and associate John
Harris, my former boss at The Economist Group David Laird,
former colleague at BT Marine Rob Struzyna and, even though
I never knew her personally, the inspiration of the late Mo
Mowlam.

There are a number of people who have helped me with my
research. Jan Abbey, Pam Hurley and everyone who gave me
feedback on the development of the survey questions helped me
to make it a great survey that has elicited useful and fascinating
insight. Karen Otazo, Jane Zirlis, Liz Luya and Paul Barlow
helped me to make sure that it reached the right people. And of
course I am also very grateful to everyone around the world who

completed the survey and who engaged in online and face-to-face conversations with me on the subject. My strengths do not run to data analysis and data presentation. Without Simon Walker and Jonathan Gulliver I would have lots of raw data and little useful insight – thank you, guys.

To a large extent it is true that the author is a book's best marketer. But in reality it takes a team of people. Nick Mannion, Julia Bezzant, the designers and my digital marketing guru Jim Banting have all been fantastic and cheered up many a tough day's writing with their emails containing cover drafts, new website designs and other exciting goodies.

My friend, writing mentor and fellow author Andy Maslen has as usual been a gem. In his 'no-holds-barred' way he has given me invaluable feedback and sound advice on the book proposal, manuscript, title and cover. Thanks, Andy – it's always educational and fun!

I am grateful to Ellen Hallsworth, my editor at Wiley, who gave me the opportunity to write this book in the first place. Thank you, Ellen, for all of your support, patience and responsiveness.

When I am juggling writing and work I am very conscious that I don't spend enough time with my precious family and friends. For their encouragement, interest and understanding I give special thanks to my mum and to my friends near and far. And to the wonderful Fi, thanks for all of your texts, your unfailing interest, wisdom and humour.

And last, but not least, thank you to my friend and partner Yannis for encouraging me to write the book and to keep going with it, for reviewing many early drafts and for general all-round unerring support and tolerance.

ABOUT THE AUTHOR

Sally Bibb is a business consultant, writer and speaker. She is co-founder of talentsmoothie, an organization development consultancy. She is also the founder of Engaging Minds, an engagement and communications consultancy. Sally's background is in international organizational change. Before setting up her businesses she was a director at The Economist Group.

Sally is the author of several successful business books, including *A Question of Trust* (with Jeremy Kourdi, 2007), *Management F/Laws* (with Russ Ackoff and Herb Addison, 2006), *The Stone Age Company* (2005), *Trust Matters* (2004 – winner of an MCA award) and *The Rookies Guide to Generation Y* (2009).

You can read more about Sally and workplace ethics at www.sallybibb.com.

INTRODUCTION

Ethics and trust are fundamental to excellent leadership and great organizations but they are often overlooked. They are invariably only treated as a priority when something goes wrong. Unethical practices in the workplace can cause irreparable damage to individuals and to the organization. Reputation, morale, productivity, loyalty, quality of work, the ability to attract the right employees and customers and ultimately profitability are all at risk in an organization that does not operate to high ethical standards. Despite these clear risks there is still not enough urgency placed on the subject. Compared to, say, the attention that executives give to the performance metrics of their organization, ethics is definitely a poor relation.

But what do we mean by ethics? It is a term that is used without us necessarily being very precise about what we are talking about. The dictionary definition of ethics is 'the rules of moral conduct governing an individual or group'. I have also asked some managers for their definition of ethics. Here are some of the answers that I have been given:

- Moral ways of doing things.
- Decisions that are based on considering others' values and what is good for them.

- At a minimum, it's following the law.
- Doing the right thing for the maximum number of people.
- The right thing to do for the most people concerned.

It is difficult to come up with a practical and all-encompassing definition of ethics but for the purposes of this book I will use the following:

- **Social** – Ethics is following social and moral obligations to a broader group of people. This means more than following the law. It means not acting in certain ways, for example lying, cheating, damaging another's property. It also means acting in certain ways, for example being honest, compassionate, listening to others' viewpoints.
- **Personal** – In order to be ethical a person needs to be aware of his or her own moral code and standards. A definition of ethics therefore has to include understanding what, as an individual, you believe to be right or wrong.

Truly ethical organizations have the opportunity to be aspired to as an employer and provider of goods and services. Think of the Fairtrade organization. It appeals to people who care about fairness and doing good and has become an aspirational brand as well as a lifestyle choice. Because ethics is part of our values it goes to the heart of our own personal identities. If we care about ethics we buy particular products and services and are loyal to certain brands not just because we need them but because doing so supports our own sense of who we are and what we care about. Organizations that create such brand loyalty are at the 'gold standard' end of the ethical spectrum. At the other end are those who pay lip-service to regulations and do the bare minimum to comply with certain ethical standards. The latter position is a short-term approach. As people become more conscious of ethical matters such organizations will lose the battle for new customers, consumers and employees to those who are genuinely committed to ethical standards and doing the right thing.

Organizations like Fairtrade are about working towards an ideal, not to a minimum standard. They are not motivated by what might happen if they get something wrong, rather by what could happen if they get things right. Such organizations are still in the minority. More organizations tend to address ethical considerations because they are motivated to prevent something bad happening. Of course it is important to acknowledge what can happen if you get it wrong. Consider the implications of ethical transgressions and you do not need to look very far to see evidence of the serious consequences of wrongdoing in the workplace. More than a handful of top executives have received prison sentences for fraudulent behaviour in organizations including Enron, Merrill Lynch, Rio Tinto, Tyco, Martha Stewart, KPMG, Credit Suisse First Boston and WorldCom. This is still relatively rare. However, what is not rare are organizational cultures that allow or encourage wrongdoing and unethical practices. Not challenging wrongdoing, allowing customers to make false assumptions, rationalizing unethical practices as well as legal infringements are to name but a few practices that over time can lead to a culture where very serious infringements are not only possible but condoned. Unethical practices, if they are not challenged, spread like viruses as they become the usual way of working. 'Everyone else does it' is a common rationalization for wrongdoing but is often a key indicator of a lack of awareness of and attention to ethical matters.

Whether you work in an organization that aspires to be ethical because it is the right thing to do or one that address ethics because of what might happen if they don't, it is increasingly important for you to get to grips with this subject and the implications for you and your business.

Irrespective of the sector you work in, ethical issues occur and they are among some of the most difficult you are likely to have to deal with.

As part of the research for this book I conducted a global survey of 315 respondents. The aim of the survey was to gain insight into respondents' attitudes to and experiences of ethics in the workplace. It is clear that dealing with ethical issues is a common demand upon people – the majority of respondents said that they had had to deal with at least one ethical issue in the previous year. Respondents had dealt with a range of ethical situations, the most common being breaches of confidentiality, bullying, dishonesty, favouritism, gossiping, not telling the whole truth and deliberately leaving out information.

As you might expect dealing with ethical issues is not an easy thing for people. Twenty-five per cent of respondents reported that one of the challenges they faced was simply not knowing how to handle the situation. Ten per cent said they did not even recognize it as an ethical issue at first and 18% said that they were worried about tackling the situation.

Not only is it one of the most challenging aspects of a person's job but there is far less attention paid to it than probably any other management skill. Doing the right thing is not always as straightforward as it seems. There are many reasons why decent people sometimes don't do the right thing. Much of the time the reasons are to do with a lack of awareness, support or skills. If you compare the investment of time and money that organizations make on training managers on budgeting, presentation skills, project management, sales and a whole range of other issues with the amount they spend on ethics training it makes no sense. Ethical wrongdoing can cost an organization a lot of money as well as put its reputation at risk, damage workforce morale and lose valuable customers. And yet most employees in most organizations are left to their own devices when it comes to handling ethical issues. Or, at best, given a code of conduct to guide them.

You would expect top management to believe that it is important for organizations to be ethical. However, some may not realize that ethics is something that they need to pay attention to and insist upon. They may think that all is well because people don't discuss ethical challenges with them. Those below top management level, however, probably have a very good feel for the nature, frequency and seriousness of ethical issues as they have to deal with them as part of their jobs. According to the survey results an overwhelming majority of survey respondents – 78% – believed that it is very important for organizations to be ethical. A number of different reasons were cited. More than 80% said that the reason for organizations to be ethical was because it is morally right. Forty-two per cent said it was important in order to avoid damaging scandals, 71% said it enhances reputation and 48% said that being ethical increases profitability. Other reasons given included complying with professional standards and obligations, ensuring a level playing field between competing businesses, maintaining employee morale, maintaining trust, providing an ethos which underpins the work of an organization, maintaining credibility with its employees, gaining the commitment of employees – because clients and customers are increasingly factoring ethical considerations into buying decisions – keeping high quality employees in your business, avoiding costly litigation, being seen as an 'employer of choice' and because unethical behaviour is infectious.

There appears to be a growing awareness of the importance of being ethical and of the consequences of getting it wrong. The media are so quick to report on ethical wrongdoing in business and politics that it would be difficult to underestimate the effect on personal and corporate reputation of being exposed as unethical.

Given the sometimes frenzied media reporting of corporate wrongdoing you may think that most people would believe that ethical standards have declined. In fact 37% thought that ethical standards had declined in the last five years while 35% of respondents thought that ethical standards in organizations had improved. It could be that the increase in regulation and scrutiny means that some believe that improvements must be taking place. Of course scrutiny and accountability are good things but there is a downside, which is that executives can lull themselves into a false sense of security by believing that if they have good regulations in place then nothing can go wrong. This is untrue of course. First, because if people are determined to get around the regulations they will, and second, because you cannot regulate everything and nor would it be advisable to try to do so. The best 'regulator' of behaviour in an organization is the culture. A culture is made up of the prevailing norms, values and practices. And these are much more powerful agents to ensure that people do the right thing than are regulations. One of the survey respondents said that in his company the following statement is sometimes heard: 'It may be unethical but it is not illegal'. If an organizational culture implicitly supports wrongdoing in day-to-day matters, regulations may prevent the big frauds but they will not stop other practices that could equally damage an organization's reputation.

If you are a manager you have a double responsibility. One is to ensure that you behave ethically yourself (bosses have more influence than they often realize in shaping others' behaviour as people tend to consciously or unconsciously copy the boss). The other is that managers are responsible for making sure that those they manage do the right thing too. A number of people surveyed said they had experience of going to their boss to discuss the particular ethical issue and their boss had advised them to leave it alone or not get involved. In a few cases people said that it was senior managers who had been guilty of unethical practice and that the justification was expedient delivery of goals. There was an understandable reluctance to challenge senior managers due to a perceived risk to the challenger and their job security. Another interesting point made was that in organizations the incentive to take the unethical option was sometimes greater than the benefit of taking the ethical one. The former route is sometimes beneficial to the individual and, according to some, there can be few perceived negative consequences. This clearly says something of the culture of the organizations where this is the case and flags up the importance of ensuring that breaches of ethical conduct do have negative consequences for the individual.

Another problem that was raised by some respondents was that they had had situations where they knew something was wrong but others put forward rationalizations as to why it was fine to do whatever had been done. They found it difficult to challenge the rationalizations.

Even if you are extremely committed to ethical practice, and are supported in doing the right thing by your organization, tackling such issues can be fraught with difficulty. It can also be a stressful and lonely business.

The survey asked people what help they had been given in dealing with ethical situations they had had to handle. Some said it was difficult to know who to turn to in such a situation. Five per cent said that they felt there was no one to turn to. The most common source of help was speaking to a friend – more people did that (26%) than spoke to their manager (21%). A few said that they consulted HR or a lawyer.

It appears that there is a worrying shortage of professional guidance as to how to handle ethical situations in organizations. Only 11% talked to a mentor, and fewer than 10% of respondents had been on a training course on ethics. Fifteen per cent said that they preferred to handle it themselves – this is clearly fine if they have the experience, knowledge and skill to do so, but organizations are leaving themselves open to a great deal of risk if this is not the case.

Given the challenges faced by people who have to deal with ethical issues coupled with the implications of getting it wrong it is surprising that organizations don't pay more attention to the subject. This can probably be explained in part by an inadequate understanding of the issues surrounding ethics in the workplace and the challenges that people face on a day-to-day basis when handling ethical situations. However, given that an organization's reputation is one of its greatest assets one would have thought that ethical practice would be as high on a chief executive's priorities as profitability. Profitability is the subject of daily attention and scrutiny in most businesses. Ethics tends only to be considered when something goes wrong.

From an individual manager's point of view, the research shows that they believe that it is important for organizations to be ethical for lots of reasons including that it is morally right. I imagine that most bosses would agree with that. However, there is still a gap between this recognition and the necessary actions being taken to make it a reality.

A solid understanding of the issues surrounding ethics, sound guidance and practical tools is needed. People need to learn how to recognize an ethical issue. They also need a good understanding of what they should do to be able to tackle ethical issues in a structured and thoughtful way, and ultimately to do the right thing.

There are a number of practical tools in this book that are intended for use in dealing with ethical issues and also in training people on the subject of ethics. They are as follows and are indicated by shading:

- Decision-making framework (Chapter 1)

- Creating an effective ethical leadership development programme (Chapter 4)
- Creating effective employees' workshops (Chapter 5)
- Creating a Code of Conduct (Chapter 5).

My aim in writing this book is to provide the understanding, insight, and, most important of all, practical guidance to help you with all manner of ethical dilemmas that you may encounter. At worst it will keep you and your organization out of trouble; at best it will mean that you get a reputation as an organization where people want to work and with whom customers want to do business. Ethics is a valuable currency whose power is much underestimated.

Read this book from cover to cover or keep it on your desk to dip into when you need it. Either way, use it to help you when you may have nowhere else to turn and to inspire you to do the right thing. I hope it helps and that you find it an enjoyable and informative read too.

CHAPTER 1

Why Ethics Matter

What this chapter will do for you:

- Give you a practical definition of 'ethics'
- Help you make sense of some of the ethical issues that you may have struggled with
- Give you a decision-making framework to use when faced with an ethical issue

WHY THIS BOOK NOW?

You are a busy executive and have lots of demands on your time. For the following reasons this book is an important one for you to dip into, read, and definitely keep on your desk to refer to when you need it.

- Many people encounter ethical issues at work and struggle to know how to tackle them.
- A practical guide can save you a lot of time as well as ensure that you have the right skills and knowledge.

- You will have the confidence that you have handled the issue well and ultimately done the right thing.
- In recent years there have been some incidents that have called into question organizations' ethics. The downfall of Enron, the scandal over the RBS chief executive's pension, UK politicians' expenses and bankers' pay have all hit the headlines around the world. This context means that the pressure on people to do the right thing and be seen to do the right thing is even greater and therefore you need to be very competent in handling ethical matters.

The majority of people in business are never given any guidance or training on ethics or ethical behaviour at work.

I wonder whether you have had any formal training or whether you have ever been in a situation where you really needed some guidance. Don't get me wrong. Most of the time people can use their own integrity and moral judgement. Mostly things work out fine.

Sometimes it's not that simple though. When ethical situations are particularly tricky some help is not only very useful but also minimizes the risk to you and the organization. Knowing that advice is at hand gives you confidence that you are making the best possible decision but also, importantly, reduces the stress involved. Ethical issues are some of the most stressful situations you're likely to encounter in your whole career as well as being those that potentially carry a great deal of risk.

My intention in writing this book is to do the following:

- Help you to handle real ethical issues in your work – and the principles will of course help you in your out-of-work life too.
- Give you practical knowledge and tools to use.
- Create a book that is easy to delve into and find help from exactly when you need it.

The style, layout and design of this book are all intended to make it easy to use as a reference guide as well as a 'cover-to-cover' read.

Ethics is a branch of philosophy and a huge and much written about field. There are some excellent books on the philosophy of ethics. This book adds to the collection because it is about the practice of ethics not the philosophy. I will briefly cover the philosophy later as it is important to understand ethical principles. But the main purpose of this book is to give you a 'how-to' guide.

The advice in this book is based on two things:

- Research into and an understanding of the practice of ethics.
- Many years of managing as well as helping others to manage in ever more complex situations and against a backdrop of seemingly falling ethical standards in business.

Knowing how to think through the issues is a key skill of ethics management. The book will help you with that thinking process. Some real examples of ethical issues faced by executives include:

- Being given information about a rival's bid in a competitive tendering process and having to make an instant judgement about whether to accept it.
- A client requesting that only male consultants work on a particular project.
- Being told by their manager to remove certain information from the results of a staff survey because it implied criticism of a senior manager.

All of these situations require making a choice which is either unethical or fraught with other difficulties and possible consequences.

The goal of this book is to help you handle ethical situations like these with confidence and clarity and ultimately to do the right thing.

The focus of the book is ethics at work, but because we are dealing with personal values and morals much of what I explore can be applied to other life situations.

But what do we mean by an ethical issue?

WHAT IS AN ETHICAL ISSUE?

Ethical issues are of course many and varied. This book is full of examples of different types of ethical issues, and how different people have responded to them at different times. An ethical issue is a situation where you are unsure about what the morally correct course of action should be. It can also be a situation where you know what you believe to be the correct course of action but to take it would result in consequences that seem in some way damaging for you or others.

When we refer to morality what we mean is a code of conduct or set of beliefs that an individual or society uses to distinguish between right and wrong behaviours.

People are usually most comfortable with a choice of two courses of action – one right and the other wrong – but ethics at work is often not that black and white. This book will help you to understand what you can do when facing issues which are not black and white but where there are shades of grey.

WHY ARE ETHICAL ISSUES SUCH A CHALLENGE FOR PEOPLE TO DEAL WITH?

Ethical issues are among the trickiest of situations for you to deal with because:

- Sometimes you don't identify problems as ethical dilemmas until it is too late.
- These situations often catch you unawares.
- You often have to think and act quickly.
- You may have little experience, knowledge, skills or confidence about how to approach the situation.

- The stakes can be high – get it wrong and people could be aggrieved and/or you could get yourself, others or the company into trouble.
- Often there is no one to turn to.

To get you into the frame of mind for thinking about such ethical issues, and the tools you can use to help you, here is one I was faced with some years ago.

A REAL-LIFE ETHICAL ISSUE
I am citing this as the first issue of the book because it contains elements that may well be familiar to you in ethical issues you have experienced:

- This problem challenged one of my personal 'rules' that I live by and thus made me really question myself.
- I had no guidance from anyone so I had to think it through myself with no knowledge or understanding of the field of ethics.
- I had no training or practical skills that I could bring to bear on the situation.
- It contained issues of the greater good versus the good of the individual.
- It contained an element of personal risk.

You may see an 'obvious' answer – in other words, to you it may be black and white. To me it wasn't because whichever course of action I chose was, I felt, 'wrong' in some way or another.

The event happened early on in my career, I had no experience of such dilemmas and I did not have a manager or mentor to turn to. The organization did not have a code of ethics – few did in those days.

Here's what happened.

I was working in an HR role and so knew lots of people in the organization, and played the role of sounding board and coach for many managers. One day a senior manager asked if she could discuss an issue with me. This was not unusual, although the nature of the issue was. Linda (not her real name) described to me how she was being treated by her boss and some of her co-workers. She was well respected by all who worked with her and had an excellent reputation in the industry. I was shocked by what she told me about how her boss and some of her peers were treating her. She described what sounded like extreme bullying and harassment and I could see she was distressed by it. Apparently the situation had been going on for some months; she was becoming more and more unhappy at work. Her husband was extremely concerned for her well-being. He was also becoming very angry about the way she was being treated and had suggested that he intervene. The situation was further complicated by the fact that he worked for a different organization, but was a big and influential player in the industry.

While Linda appreciated her husband's concerns and his desire to step in, this was adding to the pressure that she felt. She requested that I keep everything that she had told me to myself.

So what did I do? What could I do?

I asked her what she had done to try to bring an end to the way her boss and colleagues were behaving. It seemed she had done all the right things. She had told them the impact of their behaviour on her, asked them to stop, talked to her boss and told him she found his and her colleagues' behaviour completely unacceptable. She had even put it all in writing and stated that it was getting to the point where her health was being affected. All of this, she told me, took considerable guts to do but she said it had made no difference and they continued to bully her. She also told me of two other people who had told her they were being bullied by the boss.

Of course, I listened to her; I also asked if there was anything specific she would like me to do for her, but she continued to insist that she didn't want me to tell anyone about what was happening. I left that meeting with a number of concerns:

- Health – Linda was stressed and unhappy, it crossed my mind that she could even be heading for a breakdown.
- Her partner – He was an influential figure in the industry, and he was getting so angry about the way Linda was being treated that I became worried about what he might do.

- Her colleagues – From Linda's description it seemed that other staff were being bullied – there appeared to be an impact on the wider organization.
- The organization – It was a small organization with an excellent reputation in its field. Mostly people behaved very well towards one another. I was worried that Linda may be persuaded by her partner to take some kind of legal action towards the company.

This was a real ethical dilemma. I really wanted to honour the confidentiality that Linda had requested. However, I was extremely concerned about what was going on and also wanted to do what I could to fix it. It was not right that she should suffer like this at work. In addition I was well aware that as a manager myself I had moral as well as legal responsibilities to make sure the problem was resolved.

I could have really used some guidance to help me to think through the complexity of the issue and what I could do. However, even if I had not given Linda my word that I would keep this to myself, there was no one I felt I could discuss this with.

What would you do in this situation? What thoughts would be running through your head as to what your options would be?

Before I tell you what I did, let's have a look at the scenario, what I took into account (and with hindsight, should have taken into account), the options that I felt were open to me and the implications.

The facts and issues that I took into account	Options that I believed were open to me
This was clearly a case of bullying. Aside from the fact that it was morally wrong, it was against UK employment legislation.	*Tell someone senior about what was happening.* *Do nothing.*
I felt that Linda's emotional and physical health was already being badly affected. I was worried that this would worsen. I felt a moral obligation and also I felt I had a 'duty of care' to do something to stop this.	
Others were being treated this way and I did not know the effects this would have on them.	*Continue to support Linda but without telling anyone else about the situation.*
Linda's manager and the other perpetrators should be stopped before they did any more damage to people and, possibly, the company's reputation.	*Anonymously send a letter to the CEO letting him know of the situation.*
People have a right to be treated with respect at work and this behaviour was a fundamental breach of that respect.	

Possible implications

To do that would be breaking the confidentiality that I had
agreed to.

Continued damage to Linda and possible loss of her as an
employee.

A risk of her husband damaging the organization's reputation by
speaking to people he knew in the industry.

Risk of Linda quitting and bringing a case of constructive
dismissal (in UK employment law this is where an employee
resigns because of their employer's unreasonable or
unacceptable behaviour).

The risk that others would be treated like that if the perpetrators
continued to get away with it.

It may well have helped to be able to receive regular support from
a colleague but it would not have solved the problem.

I felt it would become increasingly difficult for me to continue in
this role without doing anything about the situation.

This would still be breaching confidentiality and did not sit right
with me.

It was unlikely that he would act upon the contents of an
anonymous letter.

You may well have thought of other considerations and implications. One of the things that thinking about ethics makes you realize is that as individuals, we all see things so differently. This is partly why it is so difficult to 'teach' ethics – we all have our own values, our own sense of what constitutes ethical behaviour and our own ideas on morality. This is why it is so important for organizations to train people in how to handle ethical situations and to have a code of conduct. Training can provide essential background knowledge and a structure for tackling ethical issues. And a code of conduct acts as a kind of rulebook that sets out the values and standards of behaviour that is expected of employees.

So what did I do? As I often do with difficult issues, I phoned one of my mentors. She has a lot of integrity and a strong sense of morality without being moralistic. She also has a knack of keeping things simple without being black and white. I did not feel as though I was breaking a confidence in talking to her as she was so far removed from the company. And anyway, I was well and truly stuck and to do the right thing I knew I needed to talk the situation over with someone.

My mentor asked me two questions:

- 'What do you think you should do for the greatest possible good for all concerned?'
- 'Could you live with yourself if something happened to this woman?'

She was effectively asking me to examine the consequences on all the people involved as well as getting me to think about my character. She set off a number of thoughts to do with my sense of responsibility, integrity, caring, my sense of justice and civic responsibility.

As you might expect, my answer to the second question was that I would not be able to live with myself if something happened to Linda and I would effectively be a contributor if I didn't do something. This question of the implications of not doing something is an important one for managers. Doing nothing can and has been viewed by courts as collusion with the wrongdoing. The point is – if you are a manager you have a particular responsibility for taking action to resolve the situation once you are aware of it. The harder question was what was I going to do?

I decided to speak to Linda and tell her that I was going to go to the CEO and tell him about the situation. I went to see her the next day and explained that while I respected the fact that she had asked me to keep the situation confidential I was so concerned about her and others that I felt I needed to take this action. Imagine my shock when she told me that since our meeting she had been to tell the CEO herself, as her husband had said that if she didn't, he would. I was even more shocked when she told me the CEO's response – 'I am not surprised'. Apparently the CEO had told Linda that many people found her boss very difficult and this was not the first time that he had heard of his bad behaviour. He told Linda that she was doing all the right things and she just needed to keep her head down and get on with her job. This was an interesting response and, according to the findings in the 'Ethics in the Workplace' Survey, it is not uncommon for senior management to find some way of rationalizing an ethics problem.

The CEO's response increased the seriousness of the situation. CEOs have a duty of care for their employees. His response to the situation would undoubtedly be unacceptable to a court of law.

Even if the CEO was not concerned about doing the morally right thing he needed to understand the potentially significant financial and reputational risk to the company.

With the help of my mentor I thought through what I needed to do. I clearly had to speak to the CEO and I needed to construct a compelling case for him to take action. I thought a lot about what the CEO would care about. I came up with reputation and money. I also gave some thought to why he had not taken action already. Maybe he just did not appreciate the seriousness of the situation. Maybe, because he was a tough and resilient individual, he thought that others were just as tough and able to deal with bullying. Or maybe he was nervous about confronting the manager concerned. The latter may seem like an improbable explanation. But managers, irrespective of their level in the hierarchy, often tolerate unacceptable behaviour because they are nervous of having a difficult conversation with a person. This is often the reason why unethical and inappropriate behaviour goes unchecked in organizations. And just because someone is senior does not mean that they are more prepared to have, or are skilled at, such conversations.

In order that the CEO could understand and assess the risks involved in not addressing the situation I brought in an employment lawyer. The lawyer was extremely probing and once he had heard everything we had to say he spelt out the law, how the law was apparently being broken and the risks involved to the company and the CEO of doing nothing.

To finish the story, here's what happened. The CEO spoke to Linda's boss and made it clear that his behaviour was unacceptable and had to stop. The HR director set up a chain of meetings with Linda and the others who had suffered similar treatment to that which Linda had been subjected. The goal was to find out from them what had been happening, to check that they were all right and to let them know that the company was not prepared to tolerate such behaviour. The company then created a code of conduct the goal of which was to provide guidance for people faced with such issues in the future. And, importantly, to make a public statement of the company's values and how people were expected to behave. There was a clear recognition that the company had not made it easy for Linda, her colleagues or me to put right something that was clearly wrong. And, to be fair to the CEO, he realized that he had totally mishandled the situation.

What can be learned from this situation?

There are three specific things to learn from this situation:

1. A decision-making framework or problem-solving approach would have helped me enormously. I didn't have a clear approach – I lurched from thought, emotion and idea to possible solution. It was time consuming and stressful. And at various stages of the process I was not at all sure that I had done the right thing.

2. A mentor/person to talk to inside the company would also have been helpful to help me to work through the situation clearly.

3. A code of conduct may have helped me and would certainly have provided me 'legitimacy' for raising my concerns. The following aspects of this situation would all hopefully have been covered in a code of conduct and thus would have helped me to handle the situation.

If an organization does not have a code of conduct it is effectively relying on each person to act in accordance with their own personal code of ethics or moral code. This is a risk to the organization and it puts unnecessary pressure on the individual.

DECISION-MAKING FRAMEWORK

If you don't have a framework, a mentor or a code of conduct, a checklist of questions is useful to you when faced with an ethical dilemma.

Have a look at this decision-making framework and how it relates to the Linda story above.

Decision-making framework	
Understanding the situation	Do I understand the situation?
	Have I got all of the facts and information I need?
	Are there any legal issues involved?
	What it is about the situation that I believe may make it an ethically problematic one?
	Have I looked at the situation from the perspective of all those involved?
	What is the truth of the situation?
	What is my intention?
Making the decision	Have I spoken to all of the people involved?
	What are the options?
	Are there other possibilities that I may not have thought of?
	Have I got the courage to do what is right?
	How sure am I that this is the right decision?
	What are the upsides of this decision for all concerned?
	What are the downsides of this decision for all concerned?

Continued

Decision-making framework	
Checking the decision	What are the consequences of my decision for all concerned including me, others, the company, shareholders and family and friends?
	Is my decision the right thing to do?
Acid test questions	Would I be happy for my decision to be published in the media?
	Would I be happy for my friends and family to know about my decision?
	Is there any part of me that thinks this decision is wrong or that I am ashamed of it?
	If I implement this decision is my conscience clear?
	What is the best decision for the highest possible good for all concerned?

Once someone has identified a situation as a possible ethical issue they need a structured way of thinking about it or 'interrogating' it to enable them to come to the right and ethical decision. By going through a set of questions in a structured way you have the assurance of knowing that you have considered everything that you need to consider and thought about all the angles. It helps to relieve the stress of 'have I missed something?' and/or 'I am not sure whether I am approaching this properly'. It also sets a common standard for everyone in the organization so that the overall capability of the organization is enhanced. Last but not least, should something go wrong and the organization ends up falling foul of the law, it can demonstrate that a process was in place to guard against ethical problems.

The questions are self-explanatory. The 'acid test' questions are probably the most powerful and useful. They have the effect of confirming or denying that the decision you have come to is the right one. They get people to see the much bigger perspective and also focus on whether they can do what they are planning to do with a clear conscience.

This decision making framework is invaluable for people who feel that they have an insoluable dilemma and have become very stuck. Once they have answered question five of the 'acid test' questions 'What is the best decision for the highest possible good for all concerned?' they are very clear and confident about what they need to do.

A good example of this was a consultant who had a dilemma as to whether she should break a client confidentiality agreement. She had been appointed to review the services of a healthcare service provider. As is quite standard, she was asked to sign a confidentiality agreement which stated that she should not divulge anything she found out about the company to anyone else. She discovered some practices that she believed could put people at risk in terms of their health and well-being. During the course of the project, and before she submitted her report to her client, someone in a regulatory organization who had learnt about this project telephoned her. The purpose of the call was to set up a meeting to discuss her findings as he said he had concerns about some aspects of the organization. The consultant felt in a real quandary because to her a confidentiality agreement was sacrosanct and should never be broken. On the other hand, she believed that patients were at risk and it was a serious matter. She finally came to a decision when she considered the question 'What is the best course of action for the highest possible good for all concerned?'. Her decision was to agree to the meeting with the regulator and tell him what she knew. She would forewarn her client and tell him that she felt that the situation was so serious that she had to break the confidentiality agreement.

The situation all seemed much clearer to her when she had worked through the questions. And the acid test questions gave her confidence that she was doing what she genuinely believed to be right. A word of caution though, the acid test questions are not enough on their own. You have to have the fullest possible understanding of the situation and different perspectives on it in order to make a reasonable judgement about what the best decision is in the circumstances.

The 21 question framework can also be used as the basis of a workshop where employees can practise addressing ethical dilemmas and decide what to do. It is one of the key tools needed to increase your awareness and skills in relation to ethics.

This book provides a simple analysis of the benefits of acting ethically and the implications of not doing so. It will also give you a clear understanding of why people act unethically and what the organization and its leaders can do to prevent this happening. It arms you with the knowledge and skills to identify ethical issues and gives you confidence to tackle them and to analyse the pros and cons of your decisions. Finally, it takes a look at the future of ethics and describes why the subject is likely to grow in importance in the years ahead. Ultimately the message is that if you want to pre-empt problems and stay attractive to customers and employees you need to get to grips with this subject fast.

In the next chapter we will take a look at the organizational context, how that is changing and the resulting ethical considerations.

CHAPTER 2

Developing Ethics

What this chapter will do for you:

- Help you to understand why ethical issues can be so difficult to handle and the importance of a structured approach to tackling them
- Outline the changing organizational and technological context that impact upon ethics at work
- Help you to grasp how understanding ethics could protect you from criticism
- Inspire you to learn more and develop a high level of ethical understanding and practical competence

You would probably agree that there is generally an environment of increasing mistrust towards businesses and their motives. It is unclear whether business has become more unethical over the years. But it is true that media coverage, assisted greatly by the ubiquity of the Internet, means that misdeeds are widely reported. And of course the more scandalous the cases the more they are analysed in detail by the press and the public.

It is not just the media who report wrongdoing. Citizens have now become amateur reporters. Via blogs, community groups and social networking they can also report when organizations have done something wrong.

Despite the risks involved in mishandling ethical issues, I would hazard a guess that most readers have never had a conversation with their boss about ethics. Unless you have faced an ethical dilemma you probably haven't given the subject much thought. And chances are you have never attended a training course on the subject either. The majority of the 'Ethics in the Workplace' Survey respondents believed that it was important for organizations to offer training on the subject even though most of their organizations did not offer it.

Ethical dilemmas have always been some of the toughest issues that people in organizations have to deal with. With increased scrutiny by the media, regulators and the general public there is a need to be more careful than ever. People ignore their own ethical education at their peril. Even if the organization pays no heed to its ethical responsibilities, there are clear and obvious risks for individuals not to as well, especially if you are a manager and therefore responsible for others.

On occasion business objectives and the pressure to maximize return for shareholders can mean that managers feel pressurized into not considering the ethical aspects of a given situation or decision. In fact sometimes they are actively pressurized not to do the right thing. Ultimately it is a matter of your own moral judgement.

One of the most high profile ethical dilemmas faced by a manager was that of Paul Moore, former Head of Group Regulatory Risk at the bank HBOS. In 2004 he was dismissed apparently because he told the board of the company that they were taking excessive risks. He claimed unfair dismissal and the bank settled out of court with Moore in 2005. In an interview on BBC Radio 4 Paul Moore told Michael Buerk that he decided to take the settlement money because he was thinking of his family and the impact upon them. One of the terms of the settlement was that Moore would not discuss the situation or the deal with anyone – a so-called 'gagging order'. However, in 2008 when Lehman Brothers bank collapsed Moore believed he had to act in the public interest and break the gagging order. He contacted the Treasury Select Committee and gave a testimony that he had identified 'a total failure of all key aspects of governance'. In the radio interview he said that he was not concerned about having to give the settlement money back, he was concerned that others would take revenge on him.

This is obviously an extreme case. But Moore was in a situation where he was given a choice – he could either take the money and accept the gagging order or risk taking on a large and powerful institution and those in it. According to what he has said in public since the incident, the first course of action did not sit well with him morally. When he realized that a much wider crisis in banking was occurring he felt he must blow the whistle and take the consequences.

Most managers don't have to face dilemmas with such huge public and personal consequences. Let's take a look at the kinds of situations that a manager may have to deal with and the context within which he or she is working in today's organization. Here are some real-life examples with some possible responses.

You are going to a sales meeting with a member of your team.

On the way to the meeting he says he needs to go into the local supermarket to buy a bottle of wine for the customer. He had promised to bring her a bottle of French wine from his holiday but hadn't done so. His plan was to buy a bottle from the supermarket and pretend it was from his holiday. Do you:

(a)   Say nothing. You are not happy about him lying but it's such a small thing, it doesn't matter.

(b)   Wonder whether if he would lie about a small thing like where he bought a bottle of wine from what else might he lie about.

(c)   Admire his creativity.

You are good friends with one of your suppliers. You know that he is really struggling financially at the moment as his wife has just lost her job. You notice that some of the invoices that your friend is submitting are higher than you would have expected.

No one else would know this but you are closely involved with the detail of the project that your friend is working on. Do you:

(a) Say nothing. Your friend is in need. It's such a small amount of money to the company and no one will ever find out.

(b) Have a chat with your friend and tell him that you have noticed the increase in the amount of the invoices and ask him to stop doing it. After all he is putting you in a potentially difficult situation.

(c) Tell your friend you have noticed but that if he keeps the numbers quite low you will turn a blind eye to it.

You are working late one night and notice the office administrator taking stationery from the cupboard and putting it in her handbag. What do you do?

(a) Say nothing. It's such a small thing. So many people steal office stationery it's almost like a perk of the job.

(b) It's stealing and it's not right. Let her know you have seen her take the stationery by asking her if she has lots of work to do at home.

(c) It's not right but it's only stationery – let it go but keep an eye on her.

You witness a colleague verbally abusing his secretary in the office. What's your most likely response?

(a) You think he was out of order but it's none of your business how colleagues treat their staff.

(b)   Have a quiet word with him and tell him that if you see or hear of him behaving like that again you will report him. For all you know he may treat others like that too and it is not acceptable that people should be treated like that at work.

(c)   You speak to the secretary and tell her that if it happens again she has a right to take out a grievance against her boss.

You go to a meeting with an important client. You know that the project your company is working on for the client is going really well and he is very pleased. The CEO is also pleased and has made it clear he is counting on getting more work from the same client. At the meeting the client tells you that he needs more help and asks you if any of the team is experienced in a particular area of work. It is not an area your company knows much about and there are other companies that can do it better. What do you do?

(a)   Tell him the truth and offer to find out which companies specialize in the area he needs help in. It would potentially sour the entire relationship if you took on something you were not good at.

(b)   Tell him that you can do the work and that you will get back to him with details. You are sure that you and some of your colleagues could work out what to do.

(c)   Tell him you are not sure and go and ask the CEO what
      you should do.

There are all sorts of reasons why others do not make the
choices that you may consider to be the best ones in the situations. The context and pressures at the time may well drive
people to make choices that, deep down, they consider to be
morally wrong.

It is tougher than it has ever been for people working in
organizations to try to do the right thing. Let's take a look at the
reasons why this is the case.

CORPORATE SCANDALS AND DECLINE IN PUBLIC TRUST

Based upon the number of major corporate scandals in the 2000s
it appears that there has either been a decline in ethical behaviour
in organizations or more of them are getting found out.

Nowadays we are not surprised when business or political
leaders are exposed as having broken the law or broken
ethical codes of conduct. Enron went bankrupt in 2001 as a
result of large-scale corporate accountancy fraud. WorldCom
went bankrupt in 2002 – also as a result of accountancy fraud.
Tyco bosses were convicted of theft in 2004 – the CEO and
CFO stole more than $150 million from the company. The
Royal Bank of Scotland almost collapsed in 2008 and there
followed a public outcry at the former chief executive Fred
Goodwin's pension payments. These are all examples of how far

senior leaders were prepared to go to achieve financial objectives for themselves and/or their businesses.

On a smaller financial scale, yet still an ethical issue, was the case of Abercrombie and Fitch, the clothing retailer. In 2009 one of their employees won a case of wrongful dismissal and unlawful harassment against the company after being relegated to work in the stock room because her prosthetic arm did not comply with the company's 'Look Policy'. There was a manager somewhere in that organization that enforced that policy. Maybe they agreed with it, maybe they didn't. But the fact is that every day managers have to make decisions that sometimes are in conflict with their own sense of morality.

In other cases people do things that they would not normally do but the rules or norms say that they can so they go along with it. To some extent this is what happened with MPs in the UK and resulted in such a scandal.

In 2009 the *Daily Telegraph* newspaper exposed a major-scale scandal when it obtained a copy of MPs' expenses claims and published the details. Wrongly claimed expenses included claiming for having a moat cleaned, building a duck house and other more mundane claims such as overclaiming for food and wrongly claiming expenses for second homes. This caused public outrage that lasted for months. Initially some MPs defended themselves by stating that everything that they had claimed was within the rules.

Scandals such as these have exposed political, business and public service leaders' behaviour as unethical and, in some cases, criminal. Such events have gradually eroded the public's trust in politicians, organizations and brands. In the past there may well have been a general belief that those running organizations were generally good, honest people who did the morally correct thing. Such a belief is far from universal these days. This serves to put additional pressure on managers to do the right thing and keep their organizations out of trouble.

THE GROWTH OF THE INTERNET

The subject of ethics as related to the Internet is vast and certainly worthy enough to warrant a book in itself. Like it or not, the Internet has affected people's daily lives when it comes to ethical issues and the scrutiny thereof.

Transparency

Gone are the days when organizations and managers could control the circulation of information. These days it is much easier for people to find out what is really going on and spread it around the world at the push of a button. In the past we mainly relied on company reports and the media for our information about companies. To gain the real inside information of course leaks have always been possible but nowadays it is so much easier with email and instant messaging. In 2004 Katharine Gun, a GCHQ translator in the UK, forwarded an email to a newspaper. The email contained secret information. She was arrested and charged for a breach of the Official Secrets Act. The crux of the defence was that Katharine had taken the action because she thought that the British government had acted illegally, both in taking part in the war in Iraq without UN backing, and being involved in a plot to bug UN delegates. This was a case of an employee feeling strongly about the wrongdoing of her employer and the Internet making it very easy for her to get the information to the newspapers.

The Internet and social media can also be used to rally supporters against companies. One major corporation was forced to change its plans because of the power of social networking. In 2007 blogger Lian Yue told residents of Xiamen, China, of plans to build a chemical plant in their coastal city. Opposition spread quickly via emails, blogs and texts. Before people had Internet access, construction of the factory would probably have started before the local residents knew anything about it. Even then they probably would not have known what was being built until it was finished. Although government censors shut down protesters' websites, photographs of a demonstration taken with mobile phones were sent to journalists. A million messages opposing the plan were reportedly circulated. In the end the government agreed to carry out an environmental impact study, and, as a result, the plant was moved 30 miles out of town.

If this can happen in China, it can happen anywhere. Today anyone with a mobile device and information could potentially expose a corporation and do damage to its reputation. Companies simply cannot restrict the free flow of information anymore and it's less easy for them to get away with unpopular, unethical or illegal actions.

News travels fast

Good and bad news travels around cyber space in an instant. As we saw with the Chinese chemical plant example, millions of people can get to know about problems, scandals and wrong-doings extremely quickly. Companies can no longer control what information is circulated and how fast it spreads. It also means that companies have to act very quickly in response to such viral communications. They have less time to think about their response so managers can be put under immense pressure to make decisions quickly.

In January 2010 Toyota announced the recall of over a million vehicles in the USA, Europe and China following concerns about accelerator pedals getting stuck. Akio Toyoda, the company's chief executive, was criticized for a delay in speaking to the media and making a public announcement. Mr Toyoda did eventually appear in public and made a statement and apology, but he and the company suffered even more reputation damage because he remained silent for too long.

Toyota's reaction was in total contrast to that of Jacques Nasser. He was CEO of the Ford Motor Company in 1999 when they recalled vehicles due to tyre safety problems. Ford ran a newspaper advertisement just two days after the recall and it also ran two advertuenart different commercials that showed Mr Nasser updating viewers on the recall. TV ads showed Mr Nasser telling consumers that 'over one million tires have been replaced' and he offered a personal guarantee that Ford was working hard to remedy the situation. Nasser was widely recognized by the industry for his personal integrity in the way he handled the situation, his speed of reaction and his commitment to telling the truth.

Social networking sites

Companies are now at risk of damage to their reputation and brand if people post unfavourable comments about them on social networking sites. This is a real issue for managers. Some say that social networking sites are personal matters for employees. Others cite the potential risks to their business from unfavourable comments as well as practices such as checking interviewees' profiles and using the information therein to make decisions not to hire them. A survey[1] in the USA found that 45% of them looked at job candidates' social network profiles as part of their research, and more than a third were put off hiring someone by what they saw.

Another survey[2] found that 60% of business executives say they have the 'right to know' how employees portray themselves and their organizations online, while 53% of employees contend that 'social networking pages are none of an employer's business.'

In the same survey 15% said that if their employer did something that they disagreed with they would write about it online.

Companies are struggling with this issue. Some have a strict policy on disciplining employees who are found to be complaining about their organization on websites. Others take a more enlightened view that it is best to know about problems and complaints and see it as an opportunity.

Some companies in a quest to stop employees wasting time have blocked the use of social networking sites in work time. This is short-sighted for two reasons: one is that it signals that they don't trust their employees. And if that is true, then the problem is much bigger than the use of social networking sites and the solutions lies with management's ability to build trust not to block access to such sites. The second reason why it is short-sighted is the business opportunity it poses. The connections made on such sites are helping organizations to create new business opportunities, to promote existing business and to gain knowledge and insight from far beyond the organizations' 'walls'. Of course not everyone uses social networking for these useful purposes but ignoring these potential benefits is to miss a big opportunity.

So what are the questions that a manager may have to address?

In terms of the ethical questions that people's use of the Internet raises, some of the questions that managers have to grapple with are:

- Do I have the right to know how my employees portray themselves online?
- Should I check employees' and potential employees' online profiles?
- Should I have an online profile myself and be 'friends' with colleagues and employees?
- If I do and find that, for example, an applicant posts photographs of himself drunk regularly should that be a cause of concern and if so what should I do about it?
- What shall I do if I discover that an employee has been writing negative comments about the company online?
- Should we have a company policy covering online behaviour?
- Should I accept 'friends" requests from clients on online social networking sites?
- Should I allow employees to access social networking sites in office hours?

In terms of regulating the behaviour of employees it is in part an issue of trust. Google's 'Don't be evil' policy is about the service they provide for their customers but it also about doing the right thing generally. This is a broad guideline for their employees and they trust them to use their judgement and act within that guideline. Here is a quote from their code of conduct:

We set the bar that high for practical as well as aspirational reasons: Our commitment to the highest standards helps us hire great people, who then build great products, which in turn attract loyal users. Trust and mutual respect among employees and users are the foundation of our success, and they are something we need to earn every day.

So please do read the Code, and follow it, always bearing in mind that each of us has a personal responsibility to incorporate, and to encourage other Googlers to incorporate, the principles of the Code into our work. And if you have a question or ever think that one of your fellow Googlers or the company as a whole may be falling short of our commitment, don't be silent. We want – and need – to hear from you.

That is a very clear statement of the company's intent and the responsibility that it expects all employees to take. Given this, one assumes that in Google, employees don't need to express their dissatisfaction with the company on social media sites as there is a culture where problems are taken up and sorted out internally.

Today, managers are scrutinized in ways that they have never been before. The Internet has brought a whole host of new challenges that their predecessors never had to deal with. On top of that, the public is much less trusting of organizations and is quicker to believe accusations of wrongdoing. Managers have to do all they can to ensure that they can justify their actions and decisions. These days ethical management is expected, despite the fact that most managers have had no formal education in the subject. This suggests a lack of understanding of the often complex nature of the challenge, not to mention the personal courage and commitment that it can sometimes take to tackle ethical problems. Given the personal responsibility that courts place upon executives you would be wise to ensure that you are well versed in ethics even if your organization doesn't appear to see it as a priority.

An essential part of the ethical education of managers is a basic understanding of ethical theory. The next chapter provides this essential grounding in ethics and ethical thought. It necessarily contains some philosophical background – just enough to give you the underpinning you need to be able to tackle ethical issues when they arise.

CHAPTER 3

Understanding Ethics

What this chapter will do for you.
You will learn:

- Where our own ethics come from
- Why good people sometimes do bad things
- What governs the decisions we make (sometimes without us knowing it)
- The philosophical theories that underpin ethical decisions

When we talk about ethics it's a bit like talking about love. We all have a good idea what we are talking about but perhaps have trouble articulating exactly what it means for us. Part of the skill and discipline of being a manager is to be able to understand very clearly what ethics means. This understanding will help you to make decisions yourself, to understand why others make the decisions they do and give guidance to those who work for you.

This chapter gives you the background you need. My aim is to provide you with enough so that it is helpful to you when it comes to ethical dilemmas. This means going into the philosophy a little – it is impossible to address ethics without doing this. But if you prefer the practical to the philosophical, rest assured that I am only covering the essentials and avoiding the academic.

WHY DO WE DO WHAT WE DO?

There are three primary reasons why we make the choices we make when it comes to ethics. We do what we do because of one, two or all of the following: we are obeying laws and rules, we are following social norms, or we are following our own personal moral code.

Laws and rules

Most countries have rules or laws that citizens are expected to abide by. Generally speaking they are intended to maintain order, control and harmonious living for the citizens of that country and most people abide by them. However, sometimes we may not consider laws and rules to be morally right.

An example of a law that many felt to be morally wrong was Section 28 of the UK Local Government Act 1988 which was a controversial amendment to the UK's Local Government Act 1986. The amendment stated that a local authority 'shall not intentionally promote homosexuality or publish material with the intention of promoting homosexuality' or 'promote the teaching in any maintained school of the acceptability of homosexuality as a pretended family relationship.'

This resulted in teachers and other educational staff being afraid to discuss homosexuality with students and a fear that gay relationships would be portrayed as abnormal. Many support groups closed or limited their activities as a result of Section 28. Section 28 was repealed in 2003.

Clearly this is an example that is to do with people's politics and personal beliefs. The reason it is also an ethical dilemma is because it caused individuals to make a choice about whether to follow their moral obligation to the people affected or whether to abide by the law. In examples like this, individuals risk prosecution if they ignore the law and act upon their own view of right and wrong. This is a choice many have made and risked their own freedom and lives. The most obvious examples are people who fought against apartheid in South Africa and other oppressive regimes around the world.

Thankfully most of us never find ourselves in the position of having to endanger ourselves and our families to go against the law and fight for what we believe is right. In the world of work the most that is at risk when we refuse to abide by the rules is usually our chances of promotion or our job security.

It is the leaders of organisations who have a clear responsibility for changing the rules and occcasionally even lobbying to change the laws.

Social norms and pressures

Another reason why we do what we do is because of prevailing norms or social pressures. For example, in some organizations it is the norm to discriminate against women and engage in sexist behaviour. It may be against the law and also against company policy to discriminate against women but in some organizational cultures it is accepted.

The financial services sector is notorious for its sexism. In 2009 the Equality and Human Rights Commission revealed that women earn around 80% less than men in performance-related pay at some of the UK's leading finance companies. This pay disparity is just one symptom of the much-reported sexism that exists in some financial service company cultures. Despite the fact that sex discrimination is against the law, it persists.

Women who choose to go into this working environment understand that colleagues and bosses know that the culture is likely to be more or less sexist. Even decent, respectful individuals can and do get caught up in behaving badly or just keeping their mouth shut. If you are a manager and don't speak up you are effectively condoning it because the responsibility of a manager is for a duty of care to those he or she manages. If you are not a manager and therefore have no special responsibility for others you may also feel that it is your moral duty to speak up against bad behaviour.

In the early 1980s I worked for a small shipping company. Most people there were decent and caring human beings.

Because of the naval environment most of the senior managers were men and could be described as gentlemanly and 'proper'. It was a shock when a long-standing member of staff made a claim of racial discrimination against the company. I was responsible for investigating the claim and this meant interviewing a number of his colleagues and bosses to find out what had been going on. It seemed clear that everyone liked the man who had made the claim. However, it came to light that they had given him a racially derogatory nickname. For years he had been known by this name and had not complained. It turned out that the senior managers in his work area knew about the nickname and used it themselves. Their defence was that he liked the nickname. Whether or not that was true, the fact is that senior managers had effectively condoned this kind of racially abusive behaviour. The culture in this area of the company turned out to be one that they would describe as rife with such banter but a tribunal may well have looked upon it much more negatively. The organization had an Equal Opportunities policy that forbade such behaviour but it was the norm and was part of the culture.

The company settled out of court as it was clearly culpable. While there appeared to be no malicious intent, the behaviour was deemed by the lawyers and the company as inappropriate. It highlighted a need to educate those involved as to their responsibilities as managers for the well-being of their staff, for the creation of an ethical culture and ultimately for the protection of the company's interests.

This is another example of the degree to which social norms influence decent people to behave badly. It is possible that most people feel uncomfortable with the prevailing norm but feel unable to go against the tide and challenge it.

Our own individual moral code

We each have a personal moral code. We may not think that much about it until it is put to the test but it exists. We will see later how our moral code is created. For now, let's have a look at what that means in practice.

In the absence of guidance most of us rely upon our own moral code to help us to decide what to do when we are confronted with an ethical issue.

Unless you have handled situations with ethical consequences before you probably haven't thought too much about your own moral code. Most people rely on their own sense of right and wrong and use their judgement in dealing with unfamiliar situations. For example, in deciding whether to accept a job working for a tobacco company in addition to other considerations you may well also bring your moral code to bear on the situation. Some people may not want to work for a company that produces products that damage people's health. Others may take the view that smoking is an individual's free choice and no one forces them to smoke. They may therefore conclude that working in the tobacco industry is a perfectly moral choice to make.

One management consultant may turn down a consultancy contract to help an organization that provides abortions because he or she is a practising Catholic and believes that abortions are wrong. Another may welcome such work believing that women should have free choice and that the provision of such a service is an essential one that provides freedom of choice and prevents unwanted children from being born. Such decisions are underpinned by our own moral code.

Herein lies the importance of organizations creating their own codes of conduct. Unless they are happy for managers to rely on their own sense of right and wrong the risks are evident.

WHERE DO OUR PERSONAL ETHICS COME FROM?

Most people's ethics are primarily formed as a result of the early influences of their parents or carers. This 'programming' tends to stick throughout our lives. If our parents taught us that personal privacy and respecting others' belongings is important we are likely to go through our own lives living by this 'rule'. We will be horrified if our partner opens any of our mail or reads our journal.

It is important in work and personal relationships to understand each other's values and boundaries. Without that understanding it is hard to prevent and resolve conflict and to respect one another's differences. We tend to judge ourselves by our intentions but we judge others by their behaviour. We can easily see what other people 'do'. What we can't see is the reasons why they do what they do – or their intentions. Sometimes if someone does something that we do not like or disagree with we don't stop to think about why they have done it. They may have a perfectly good intention. A young graduate may reply to an email sent by the CEO saying that he totally disagrees with a business decision announced in the email. The graduate's intention may be very positive – he loves the company and wants it to do well. What is more the CEO has said that he has an 'open door policy' and staff should be encouraged to say what they think. The CEO, however, who is in his late fifties, judges this behaviour as inappropriate and lacking political awareness. He himself would never have dreamt of challenging the boss when he was in his twenties. He is judging the graduate on his behaviour which he deems to be inappropriate. He does not know that the intention behind the behaviour is extremely positive.

Our personal moral code is also shaped by people other than our parents. Sometimes people change their perspective on something as a result of encountering another influential person who they see as a role model. Often it is a case of them not having realized that there was a different way to think about the situation. For example, Bob has a colleague called Angela. Angela has a very difficult colleague (Mary). The two of them did not get along at all. Bob would receive phone calls from Mary who would ask questions about what Angela was thinking of doing, where she was and how happy she was. Bob thought he was helping by telling her all this information. Bob's intention was to try to help by 'fixing' the situation between these two women. He thought that keeping lines of communication open with Mary would mean he would eventually win her trust and somehow help them solve their relationship conflicts. Another way of looking at the situation is that he was potentially breaking confidences and risked losing Angela's trust. While his intention was to help he was strongly driven by his own need to fix other people's problems. It took someone else to point this out to Bob before he realized that what he was doing may not have been acceptable to others.

Bob realized that his parents were the type of people who always took it upon themselves to try to fix others' problems. He had grown up thinking that that was the caring thing to do. Of course that may sometimes be the case. But the point is that his way of operating had been challenged by someone and it caused him to think differently about something that he had learnt from his parents and never questioned.

If you are a manager and you have, or have had, an excellent role model, you are lucky. It's useful, even if the person is not available to talk to, to ask yourself, "what would x person say about this situation?"

I learnt a lot from a man who was my mentor for many years. I observed him in some very challenging situations. I also discussed with him how to handle situations where I was not sure what to do. He rarely told me what he thought I should do but he asked me all the questions I needed to be asked in order to find a solution that I felt to be the right one. This is what a good mentor can do. It is a useful process as it makes our own values transparent to ourselves and allows us the choice of approaching something differently and with a greater range of choices at our disposal.

As well as the early influences on us, our character is also a strong determinant of our ethics. It could be said that our character is who we are when no one is looking. It's a good way of looking at it, because it goes beyond how we like to think we come across to others. Our character is made up of a number of traits that underpin our conduct: trustworthiness, caring and independent thought.

Being trustworthy and trusting is at the core of ethical character. There are a number of components of trust, or reasons why others trust us. A person might instil trust because of some or all of these components. It is important to break down trust in this way so that we can understand specifically what it is about us and what we do that makes others trust us. That way we can spot any deficit areas and set about fixing them. Let's take a look at each component:

- Capability – whether they have the skills, competence, professional reputation and experience needed in the particular context or situation.

- Predictability – or whether another person can foretell how we are likely to behave in a commonly experienced situation. For example, you may know that a colleague will arrive at work at 9 am. This is when he usually arrives and, barring circumstances out of his control, he will always arrive at 9 am.

- Reliability – this is about dependability and taking responsibility. Nine times out of ten you know your colleague will arrive at 9 am. When he doesn't arrive on time he is no more than five minutes late or you know that something has happened that is out of his control and he is unable to call you for some reason. Taking our responsibilities seriously and keeping promises is part of reliability. Reliable people do not take on commitments that they do not think they can meet. And they don't make excuses in the event that they break a commitment. Reliability is also about being clear with yourself and others what you are committing to do.

Capability, predictability and reliability are straightforward and easy to understand. The fourth component, integrity, is more complicated as it is made up of a number of factors so we need to break it down and look at each one in turn.

The dictionary definition of integrity is 'soundness of moral character'. This is rather vague though. It is useful to break down integrity into its component parts if we are to understand and ultimately try to improve our integrity.

The first thing that comes to mind when you consider what integrity means is honesty. I would argue that it also incorporates the following: sincerity, empathy, congruence, humility and courage. Let's take a look at each of these and what they actually mean.

Honesty means telling the truth, the whole truth and not knowingly allowing people to be misled. Being truthful is about presenting the situation in as factual a way as we can. It also means not keeping quiet when it is clear that others have misunderstood, not knowingly allowing people to make false assumptions and not telling the whole truth. Importantly it is about *intent*. There may be situations when not telling the truth is important for the greater ethical good, for example a police officer going undercover to break a drugs ring. In this case the intention is an ethical one even though lies may be told.

Sincerity is about being genuine and believing yourself what you are saying to another. It is about not making out-of-context statements or being silent with the goal of misleading. For example, a person who is working on a project that is likely to get him a promotion is being insincere when he says to his team in a project review meeting: 'There is nowhere else I would rather be right now.' In saying that, in his circumstances, he is being insincere because he is misleading them into believing that he wants nothing more than to be working with them whereas what he actually wants is the benefits that the project will bring him, i.e. a promotion.

Empathy is the capacity to appreciate a situation from another's viewpoint. Empathy is important because it means you are interested in what it's like to be in others' shoes. This enables you to truly take into consideration their perspectives.

Congruence is another important component of integrity. Congruence is when your beliefs, words and actions all match. A great example of congruence was Mahatma Gandhi when he was invited to speak before the House of Commons. He spoke for two hours without notes and received a standing ovation. Afterwards his secretary was approached – she was asked why he could speak for two hours without notes. Her reply was 'What Gandhi thinks, what he does and what he feels are all the same. He does not need notes. When you consistently demonstrate inner congruence to your beliefs and principles you inspire trust. People feel you are strong solid and dependable.'

Humility is about being concerned about doing what is right rather than *being right*, about *acting on* good ideas rather needing to *have* the good ideas, about taking on board new truths rather than defending old positions and about recognizing contribution rather than needing to be recognized. When Jim Collins researched[2] good companies that transformed to great companies he found to his surprise that all the companies had what he described as 'Level 5 leadership'. These leaders were not the celebrity leadership types, they were a paradoxical blend of personal humility and professional will. He found that the humble leaders stood firmly for principle even in the face of opposition. They didn't get caught up in arrogance, manipulation, power games or bravado. It didn't mean that they were weak, reticent or self effacing. It did mean that they 'looked into the mirror when things went wrong and out of the window when things went right'.

Courage is doing the right thing even when it's hard. Courage is an important component of integrity because it is sometimes necessary to speak up, even when there may be personal risk in doing so. Courage is definitely a trait that is needed when dealing with tough ethical situations. In the 'Ethics in the Workplace' Survey 2010 20% of respondents said that one of the challenges they encountered in dealing with ethical situations was being worried about possible negative consequences on their career. 18% said that they were worried about tackling the situation. If people feel like this about dealing with ethical issues it is clear that courage is a quality that is needed and should not be underestimated.

As we have seen, integrity is an essential component of trustworthiness. Without integrity, even if you are capable and reliable, you will not be trusted. As Warren Buffett, the investor, businessman and philanthropist, said: 'I look for three things in hiring people. The first is personal integrity, the second is intelligence, and the third is a high energy level. But if you don't have the first, the other two will kill you.'

Let's have a look at the two remaining components of an ethical character: caring and independent thought.

Caring is important. It is not possible to have an ethical character without caring. Caring for others and wanting the right thing by them is at the heart of ethics. Caring for the people, the outcomes and the greatest possible good for all concerned are all essential components. That doesn't mean that sometimes it isn't necessary to hurt people in order to be ethical. For example, turning someone down for a job when that is the best decision may hurt them but it is still ethical. Caring about how you handle that is the concern of a person with ethical character. Essentially caring people feel some emotional response to the hurt and pain of others. For a manager or someone who is responsible for seeing that ethical practice takes place it is essential to be caring. Selfishness and not caring about others (stakeholders, customers, colleagues) is at the root of corporate scandals and bankruptcies.

Finally, a person of ethical character has independence of thought. This is the ability to act according to your own beliefs irrespective of the context you find yourself in. This character trait is underpinned by courage which is essential if you are going against peers or bosses or social norms in order to do what you believe is right. I have known managers who I considered to be very ethical people but who struggled to carry out the courage of their convictions if it meant going against authority.

WHY GOOD PEOPLE DO BAD THINGS

Even people with good ethical character can be derailed by the context they are in and the pressures that that can impose. Probably one of the most famous pieces of research that proves this was carried out by Stanley Milgram, a professor at Yale University, in 1960. Milgram wanted to study the conflict between obedience to authority and personal conscience. He studied the justifications for acts of genocide by those accused at the World War Two Nuremberg Trials. Their defence was often based on obedience to authority, i.e. they were told to do what they did by their superiors.

Milgram set up an experiment to find out whether and to what extent people would be prepared to inflict harm on others if told to do so by an authority figure.

Participants were told that the experiment was investigating the effects of punishment on learning behaviour. There were two sets of subjects – the apparent subjects and actual subjects. The actual subjects were not aware that it was they who were actually being studied.

The apparent subjects (who were actually actors) were wired up and would pretend to receive an electric shock each time they (the actual subjects) pushed a button. The actual subjects believed that the electric shock was real.

Milgram told the participants to administer electric shocks every time the person got a quiz question wrong. They were told that if they did not continue to administer shocks they would spoil the experiment. Despite the screams of pain, the real subjects continued to administer the shocks when the 'authority figure' in a white coat told them to. 60% of them obeyed orders to punish their 'victim' to the very end of the 450-volt scale. None of them stopped before reaching 300 volts.

Milgram concluded that 'ordinary' people were capable of committing horrendous acts if they were told to do so by authority figures. Their sense of 'is this right?' becomes overridden by 'this is what this authority figure wants me to do'. Milgram summarized the experiment in his 1974 article, 'The Perils of Obedience', writing:

> Ordinary people, simply doing their jobs, and without any particular hostility on their part, can become agents in a terrible destructive process. Moreover, even when the destructive effects of their work become patently clear, and they are asked to carry out actions incompatible with fundamental standards of morality, relatively few people have the resources needed to resist authority.

In organizational contexts, particularly ones that are characterized by a rigid hierarchy, the risk of good people doing bad things is real because the nature of a hierarchy is that everyone except those at the top has authority figures above them. Even where there isn't a formal hierarchy, people naturally locate themselves in relation to others. This means that they are susceptible to the demands of those whom they perceive as being in some way 'superior' to them and having authority over them.

In addition to the pressures of the hierarchy, people end up doing bad things because there is no single 'right' course of action. So decent people can end up doing something 'wrong' because they have to effectively make a choice between wrong and wrong. Then you have to decide which course of action is less wrong. Michael Sandel is a political philosopher and professor at Harvard University. He gives a very popular course called 'Justice' whose aim is to explore moral dilemmas and get the students thinking about ethics and morality.

Professor Sandel poses this question on the first day of the course. You are driving a trolley car when the brakes fail. You notice five men working on the track ahead of you. You will certainly kill them. You then notice that you could steer the trolley onto another track where you will kill only one worker. You have seconds to make the choice. 'What would you do?'

Whatever decision a student offers, there is at least one more student with a reasonable argument against it. And when they offer their own decision and rationale, there is of course someone who argues against them. A popular argument is that you should not actively do anything – in other words you should allow the trolley car to go where it was going to go anyway and kill the five men. Intervening is somehow wrong because you are then making a conscious decision to kill one person. It is of course a condundrum for which there is no 'right' solution.

Professor Sandel then presents the students with an alternative scenario. You are standing on a bridge overlooking the track. You could save all six workers by pushing that fat man standing next to you into the trolley's path. This causes visible discomfort among some students. Some of them think it is wrong to push someone off a bridge. Inflicting harm on someone using their own hands feels really wrong. 'So,' Sandel continues, 'what if you didn't actually have to push the fat man but could drop him through a trapdoor by pulling a lever?'

As you can imagine, this class causes a great deal of torment to the poor students who cannot find the 'right' answer. Of course there is no right answer there are only different ways of viewing the situations. This is the preserve of moral philosophy. Moral philosophies are the principles that underpin our ethical choices. Most managers have probably never been taught them even though they will have used them implicitly all of their lives. Along with our moral character, they are the determinants of the ways we approach ethical situations.

There are a number of ethical doctrines or philosophies that underpin our thinking when we make ethical choices.

THE PHILOSOPHICAL DRIVERS OF OUR ETHICS
Whenever we are making ethical choices, whether we know it or not our actions can be associated with one of the main ethical

theories. Understanding these theories is not essential but it is useful as it provides an underpinning for the practical tools we will look at later in this book.

The ethical theories are derived from the works and thoughts of a number of key philosophers. Philosophical theories are complicated and you may not have the time or inclination to study them in all their complexity. So I have distilled the theories to give you the essential insights that are relevant to making good, practical decisions.

There are three major theories that are helpful to understand – utilitarianism (or the ethics of *consequences*), deontology (or the ethics of *duty*) and virtue ethics (or the ethics of *character*).

Utilitarianism

Utilitarianism is concerned with *consequences* and the course of action that benefits the greatest number of people, irrespective of who those people are. Impartiality is key according to utilitarianism. One must not favour friends or family. And the moral worth of an action is solely determined by its outcome. The main two proponents of utilitarianism were Jeremy Bentham (1748–1832) and John Stuart Mill (1806–1873). Jeremy Bentham's assertion was that the best consequences were those that resulted in the most amount of pleasure. This branch of utilitarianism is known as *hedonistic utilitarianism*. John Stuart Mill, on the other hand, argued that the best consequences are the ones that create the most *happiness*.

This branch of utilitarianism is known as eudaimonistic utilitarianism.

Utilitarianism is distinct from all other ethical theories because consequences are all that matters when making an ethical decision. It doesn't matter, for example, whether you lie. The only thing that matters about lying is the consequence of doing so. So, for example, imagine you are an excellent teacher who has had good results and testimonials but no university degree. You apply for a teaching job and one of the criteria is a university degree so you lie on your application form and say that you have a degree. That is a utilitarian decision because the thing that matters is the consequences, i.e. that many children receive the benefit of being taught by an excellent teacher. It does not matter that you have lied to get the job. In other words, the end justifies the means.

I experienced this approach first hand recently in an encounter with a shop assistant. The advice she gave me followed utilitarian principles although I am sure she didn't know it. I went into the shop to buy a new hands-free set for my mobile phone as I had lost mine. They didn't sell them in the shop and she advised me to phone the company who would be able to supply one. She went on to tell me not to say that I had lost it but to say that it had broken and then they would probably send me a replacement free of charge. She was obviously trying to be helpful and give me the outcome that I wanted. Advising the customer to lie to her employer obviously was not a problem for her.

Utilitarianism does, on the face of it, have its appeal. It's always good to consider consequences and to try to achieve the best consequences for those concerned. However, as you have probably worked out by now, there are problems with utilitarianism. It is often not so simple to work out which course of action has the best consequences for the most number of people. Also, how do you define what the best consequences are? Is it to make them happy or to increase their pleasure, or do what you judge to be good for them in some other way – perhaps to increase their health, their wealth or power? And how do you assess the consequences on others? In a complex world and in dealing with complex situations it is of course impossible to know all possible consequences on others, let alone to assess those consequences. Sometimes, as in Professor Sandel's trolley car example, no matter which course of action you take there will be people who will lose out in some way.

So you can see that while thinking about consequences of actions is important there is more to ethical decision making than that.

Deontology

In contrast to utilitarians, deontologists argue that the ends do not always justify the means. The word 'deon' is Greek and means *duty* or *obligation*. For deontologists only the act is important not the consequences or our intentions. For example, lying is always wrong. Even, say, lying to the Nazis that you were hiding Jewish friends in your house to protect them would be considered wrong by a deontologist. The German philosopher Immanuel Kant asserted that the consequences of our actions never matter. Others believe that we should consider consequences *and* duty. Kant held that it was wrong to consider human beings as a means to an end. In other words, we should never treat people as though they are just a mechanism to achieve something.

W.D. Ross (1877–1971) was a Scottish professor. He made a useful contribution to ethics in general and deontology in particular by introducing the idea of prima facie obligations. He identified seven prima-facie obligations which guide a person as to what they should do in any given situation. Beneficence (or the duty to help other people), non-maleficence (a duty to avoid harming other people), justice (a duty to help people to get what they deserve), self-improvement (a duty to improve ourselves), reparation (a duty to compensate someone if you have acted wrongly towards them), gratitude (a duty to help others who have helped us) and promise-keeping (a duty to keep implicit or explicit promises to others include telling the truth). Ross said that when a person was considering a course of action he or she should consider all of these prima facie duties. He also argued that there was no such thing as a true ethical dilemma; it was only a question of deciding which of these prima facie obligations is the most important in any given situation. For example, you may have promised your child you would take them to the cinema but a friend phones and tells you she is seriously ill and needs you to take her to the hospital. In this case you would decide that breaking your promise to your child is over-ridden by the importance of taking your friend to the hospital.

The problem with deontology is that the morally correct course of action is subjective. There is of course no universally agreed set of rules so from a practical perspective, deontology has limited usefulness.

Both utilitarianism and deontology are focused on the action that occurs as a result of an ethical decision. There is another theory that is focused not on the action we take but on the person we are. Virtue ethics asks not 'what should I do?' but 'who should I be?'

Virtue ethics

The roots of the philosophical thought behind virtue ethics come from Aristotle and Plato. Virtue ethics can sit alongside utilitarianism and deontology as it is concerned with a person's character not with what they decide to do. Aristotle identified 12 moral virtues. He said that each of these virtues were the middle ground between two extreme vices –deficiency and excess. He believed that we must learn to regulate our behaviour and find a middle ground between the two extremes. The 12 virtues and their correspondent extremes are: courage (the middle ground between cowardice and rashness), temperance (between temperance and insensibility), liberality (between illiberality and prodigality), munificence (between vulgarity and pettiness), high-mindedness (between humility and vaingloriousness), right-ambition (between overambition and want-of-ambition), good temper (between spiritlessness and irascibility), friendly civility (between surliness and obsequiousness), sincerity (between ironical depreciation and boastfulness), wittiness (between boorishness and buffoonery), modesty (between shamelessness and bashfulness), just resentment (between callousness and spitefulness).

Aristotle argued that practising these virtues led to a proper moral life. The idea of practising is an important one in virtue ethics. The argument goes that in order to live a virtuous life each of the virtues needs to be practised regularly. Just as virtues are habitual, so are vices and the difference between the two is that one leads to human suffering and the other does not. Here again we hit upon the issue of subjectivity. There is no rulebook that tells us what leads to suffering and what doesn't. It all comes down to our judgement. It is also a question of context. What is considered a virtue in one culture may not in another culture. In some societies, what is considered a virtue differs between men and women.

Virtue ethics is also flawed in that it tries to separate our character from our actions. These two are inseparable because at times we need to consider the consequences of our actions in order to figure out what virtue we need to practise to cause the best possible outcome.

HOW DOES A KNOWLEDGE OF THE ETHICAL THEORIES HELP TO GUIDE DECISION MAKING?

It is probably fair to say that the majority of managers don't know about or understand the ethical philosophies. However, most of us probably mainly act in accordance to one of them in particular.

Consider the situation I described above of the shop assistant advising me to lie and say that my headset had broken in order that I would be sent a replacement. If her manager's perspective was a deontological one he may well have fired her because lying is always wrong. However, if he considered a utilitarian perspective he may well come to the conclusion that the consequence, i.e. I received a new headset, meant that her advice was right because the customer got what she wanted.

Smart decision making can only be done by understanding the different perspectives and therefore the options open to you. Understanding these perspectives and options helps you to appreciate the reasons why you may clash with others on ethical questions. In other words, they have a different perspective which you may previously have thought invalid but understanding the principles behind it helps you to understand.

An increase in knowledge in this field helps you to make informed choices and also to understand clearly the rationale for the decisions that you make and the options that you have considered but rejected.

The diagram below shows that if you have low awareness and apply little or no analysis you will be stuck in indecision. If you apply lots of analysis without awareness you will make unwise decisions, if you have high awareness but apply little analysis you will make blind decisions. The ideal spot to be in is the top right-hand corner where you have high awareness and high analysis, the result of which is smart decision making.

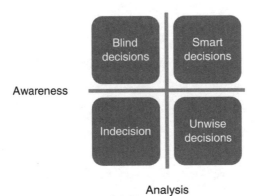

Understanding what drives your own and other people's behaviour, particularly the influence of character and authority figures, is crucial. Only then can you really have a chance of influencing those drivers and making the best ethical choices possible and helping others to do so.

Understanding the moral philosophies can help you in a practical way too. Seeing another ethical perspective helps to open up possibilities and even become less judgemental of people who have a different moral code from your own.

In the next chapter we are going to take a look at the powerful role a leader has in creating ethical organizations and the huge benefits of getting it right.

CHAPTER 4

The Ethical Leader

What this chapter will do for you.

You will learn:

- The benefits of ethical leadership
- The importance of the culture set by the leader
- The characteristics of an ethical leader
- How to develop ethical leaders

WHAT IS ETHICAL LEADERSHIP?

The top leaders of organizations are the role models. It is what they do not what they say that people take notice of. If a leader has high ethical standards and demonstrates these, say in his lack of tolerance for wrongdoing, others will understand that what they do should live up to these standards.

One CEO, David (not his real name), told me the story of how he dismissed an employee who had worked for the company for 20 years. When David was appointed CEO he started to hear disturbing stories from a number of sources about one of the top performing sales people. This man had threatened and coerced other employees and some external partners to do what he wanted them to do. David found this behaviour totally unacceptable and inexcusable. He consulted with his lawyer because he intended to dismiss the man. The lawyer advised him that unless he followed the company's disciplinary process he ran the risk of losing a case of unfair dismissal which he estimated could cost around £50,000. To David this was a small price to pay. He called the salesman into his office, told him he was dismissed and personally accompanied him to his office to collect his belongings and then to his car. He sent him home never to return. The reason he did this personally was because he expected the man to make threats. Indeed he did threaten David and a number of other people; he also sued the company for unfair dismissal. As the lawyer predicted, they lost the case because they had not followed a due process. They had to pay more than £50,000 in compensation. To David it was worth it. A number of people, both internal and external, came to see David and regaled him with tales of how for years this man had made their lives a misery.

Importantly, the other senior managers started to tackle cases of misconduct that they previously said they had been nervous to address because they were afraid that they wouldn't get the company's backing. David told me that he wouldn't have dreamt of *not* tackling the situation. By tackling it in such a clear and decisive way, he set the standard that he expected and sent a strong signal that he would not tolerate abusive behaviour. His actions also made it clear that no matter how much revenue an individual brought in they would not be excused bad behaviour.

Many CEOs would not have sacked such a high-earning salesman. Not doing so, however, sends a strong message that the means justify the ends. And this is the reason why so many badly behaved individuals get away with behaviour that is wrong but makes the company money.

CEOs like David have a moral code that they follow. During the interviews for this book they often referred to their upbringing and having their values instilled in them early in life. They put the interests of the organization and its people before their own and doing the right thing is important to them. All of the CEOs I interviewed had built very successful enterprises. The conversations we had about leaving a legacy and instilling moral values was probably not the kind of conversation that anyone would have had with the people who presided over organizations like Enron and RBS.

THE CORE PURPOSE OF BUSINESS: TO CREATE SHAREHOLDER VALUE OR TO SERVE THE GREATER GOOD?

Leaders of businesses and other organizations are increasingly waking up to the reality of organizational ethics. The cynics might say that this is not driven by some desire to be good. Rather that there is so much pressure to be seen to be doing the right thing. Public opinion, which is now easily accessible via the Internet, is reshaping expectations and standards. The Internet also means that the behaviour of those in charge of organizations is more visible than ever. Injustice anywhere in the world is becoming more and more visible, more subject to scrutiny and less and less acceptable.

In an article for the *Harvard Business Review*[1] the authors talked about how the performance of leaders has traditionally been evaluated, that is by the extent to which they created wealth for investors. They argue that we need a better way and propose 'the extent to which executives create organizations that are economically, ethically and socially sustainable.'

Business schools' teachings are still very skewed towards the idea that increasing shareholder value is the *raison d'être* of business. However, there are changes afoot.

In the past business school professors and business leaders have tended to subscribe to the economist Milton Friedman's view that the only responsibility of business is to maximize profits. A small but probably significant testimony to this new way of thinking was the actions of the Harvard Business School's MBA graduates of June 2009. They created a ceremony at the time of their graduation where they promised they would 'serve the greater good,' 'act with the utmost integrity,' and avoid 'decisions and behaviour that advance my own narrow ambitions, but harm the enterprise and the societies it serves.' It appears that the new generation of MBA students wants to distance itself from the questionable morals and actions of its predecessors on whose watch the financial crisis of 2009 occurred. The financial crisis and subsequent economic recession have prompted a much greater degree of scrutiny of organizations and those who lead them. An oath like the one created by the Harvard Business School graduates may be indicative of a new generation of managers who are committed to actively managing ethically and being seen to do so.

All generations of business leaders and heads of organizations are now at least aware that there is a call for expanding the goals of business beyond just creating wealth for investors.

This is a big leap in mindset for some leaders. Intellectually the argument for ethical and socially responsible business is not difficult to grasp. Nor perhaps are some of the actions needed in the business to make them a reality. The first step is to convince themselves that there are benefits beyond just being ethical for the sake of it. There are leaders who believe that there is no other way to be. They are people with high moral standards. Then there are those who have less of an innate moral driver. They don't have a natural orientation towards ethical leadership and need to see clear and logical benefits.

THE BENEFITS OF ETHICAL BUSINESS

Ethisphere, a think-tank specializing in ethics, publishes an annual 'World Most Ethical Companies Ranking'.[2] Entrants are scored in seven categories: Corporate Citizenship and

Responsibility (20%); Corporate Governance (10%); Innovation that Contributes to the Public Well Being (15%); Industry Leadership (5%); Executive Leadership and Tone from the Top (15%); Legal, Regulatory and Reputation Track Record (20%); and Internal Systems and Ethics/Compliance Program (15%).

'Leadership and Tone from the Top' make up 15% of the total score that an organization can achieve. I would argue that all the other categories flow from it and that leadership is the most important and influential determinant of ethics in an organization. The other categories are influenced by the person in charge. There is no getting away from the fact that the person at the top sets the standard of behaviour throughout the entire organization. They have the opportunity to place the highest premium on ethics if they choose to.

Because of an increase in known corporate misdeeds and subsequent scandals in the 1990s and early 2000s leaders who were not naturally inclined to be of high ethical character ran more risk of being exposed for failures of integrity. Ethical behaviour is now on the agenda of many of these leaders because they see the downside of not paying attention to it.

- *Competitive advantage* – Consumers are increasingly favouring companies that demonstrate ethical practices. Failure to do so means lost market share, shrinking popularity and bad PR, all of which can affect revenues and profits.

- *Investment* – Investors are becoming keenly aware that it makes sense to invest in organizations that are scandal-free and are run with integrity because of the implications of being associated with unethical practice.
- *Better staff attraction and retention* – Increasingly, people want to work for ethical employers. In the 'Ethics in the Workplace' Survey[3] 70% of respondents said that having top management who demonstrate high standards of ethics is important. Around 40% said that top management in their organization do so.

  Organizations that have been exposed for wrongdoing damage their ability to attract recruits. On the other hand, organizations that are seen to do good work, treat consumers fairly and provide a great place to work, have no trouble attracting the best talent.

- *Morale and culture* – People who work in an ethical, high-integrity organization tend to appreciate it and be proud of the fact. The atmosphere is open and unsuppressed and the culture is much more pleasant as a result. Employees become advocates for the organization and thus attract more good people to work there.
- *Reputation* – It takes years to build organizational reputation but only one scandal to destroy it. Ethical organizations are far less prone to scandals and disasters. And if one does occur, an ethical organization will deal with it quickly and honestly. People tend to forgive organizations who are

genuinely trying to do the right thing. People do not forgive organizations who fail and then fail again by not addressing the problem and the root cause. The public gets very angry with corporate leaders who appear on television after a disaster and don't own up, who try to spin the truth or, worse, deny what has happened.

- *Legal and regulatory reasons* – Standards and compliance mechanisms are becoming commonplace. Transparency and accountability are now part of the regulatory environment. But ethical practice goes far beyond compliance and regulations are not enough to create an ethical culture.

- *Legacy* – some leaders are motivated by furthering their own ambitions – whether it be increasing their power, financial wealth or both. The higher class of leader is motivated by deeper aspirations – by leaving some kind of legacy and doing the right thing. While these kinds of leaders have always existed, in the future, their attitude will be a differentiator and organizations will increasingly look to hire people like them. Ethical leaders have the best interests of the organization at heart, not their own best interests.

Jim Collins identifies this category of executives as Level 5 Leaders: leaders who are able to 'channel their ego needs away from themselves and into the larger goal of building a great company.'

These kinds of leaders are the ones that organizations increasingly want to hire.

THE POWER OF THE LEADER

It is becoming more and more common for organizations to run ethics programmes to instil in people good behaviour. Such courses are useful but only if the context is one that rewards ethical behaviour and punishes unethical behaviour. That may sound extreme, but research has shown that it is a waste of time trying to reform errant individuals if the organizational context allows or encourages bad behaviour.

The social psychologist Philip Zimbardo conducted a now famous experiment that demonstrated the power of context very well. At the University of Stanford in 1971 he assigned a group of men to the role of prison guards and another group were assigned as inmates. Zimbardo had to halt the experiment when the guards started to physically and emotionally abuse the inmates. Upon analysing the behaviour displayed in this experiment and in situations such as the holocaust where people did terrible things to others, Zimbardo concluded that most people have the capacity to do bad things if the situation and system encourages or pressurizes them to do so. He argues that the context is a far greater determinant of behaviour than an individual's character. As we saw in Chapter 3, Stanley Milgram's work demonstrated that human beings have an inbuilt desire to belong and a fear of challenging those in authority. Organizations have systematized conformity because of their hierarchical nature and pressure not to challenge those in power. In organizations even the strongest and most principled people can and do commit acts that you would not normally expect them to.

So what does this tell us about the importance of leadership in organizations? The message is clear. Leaders should pay close attention to the culture that they are creating because context is the key determinant of people's behaviour. The leader needs to model everything that he or she wants to see in others. Like it or not, the boss holds an enormous amount of power. That power can be used to create an environment where people do the right thing most of the time, or it can be used to ensure that people conform.

Bob Galvin, former CEO of Motorola, understood the importance of an egalitarian organizational culture where people felt a sense of ownership and could speak their minds. A story that nicely illustrates Galvin's approach is one of a young middle manager who disagreed with a decision Galvin had taken, went to see him and told him: 'Bob, I heard that point you made this morning, and I think you are dead wrong. I'm going to prove it. I'm going to shoot you down.' Apparently the young man stormed off and Galvin proudly announced to a colleague: 'That's how we've overcome Texas Instruments' lead in semi-conductors.' This was in the 1980s and the company was doing really well. At that time managers got ahead by actively challenging the status quo. Galvin's view was that he was not the smartest person in the company, and that the company's success was due to the fact that he had surrounded himself with mangers more talented than he was who were prepared to challenge him.

There is a fair chance that you have never come across a CEO like Bob Galvin. Many leaders value the privilege of power and the compliance that others show in the face of that power. Employees are afraid to challenge and simply want to please the boss. In fact middle managers can and do put the health of the organization at risk in order to toe the line. It is not just that they are afraid to challenge. They also at times wrongly pre-empt their boss's wishes. Junior or middle managers are so keen not to rock the boat or to please their bosses that they take the path of least resistance. Whether or not their actions or decisions are in the best interests of the organization is irrelevant. A management consultant experienced this first hand in an interesting and tricky situation she encountered with a client.

She had been asked to carry out a piece of research into the culture of the organization – it involved talking to several hundred employees to find out what they liked and disliked about the company and what they thought got in the way of good business.

She prepared a report that detailed all of the feedback, good and bad. Her client was a middle manager who was clearly worried about presenting any 'bad news' to his boss and was worried about the implied criticism of some senior managers. So he requested that all the negative comments be removed from the report. In fact his boss was particularly interested in the negative comments because he was working with the CEO to try to change the culture to a much more entrepreneurial one and wanted to understand what was getting in the way. The middle manager did not know this and basically wanted to 'cover up' the bad news presumably out of fear that he would be an unpopular messenger. His manager made the mistake of not making it clear that he would reward 'truth-telling' and, as he later told the consultant, 'courageous action.'

It is frightening that irrespective of the seniority of managers or how much they are paid to do their job, fear of challenging those in power can stop them from doing the right thing and sometimes mean they do the absolutely wrong thing. This is a serious malaise in organizations. It is all the more serious when people accept it as part and parcel of organizational life and see unhealthy compliance as loyalty thus rendering it acceptable.

I have been astonished on many occasions to find that CEOs and bosses of large organizations totally underestimate the power they hold. They do not appreciate that everything that they say and do is a signal to those in the organization as to how they should behave. The single most effective way of creating an ethical culture is to have a CEO who lives and breathes ethical behaviour and lets people see him doing so in actions as well as words. A CEO who has zero tolerance for any unethical practices quickly signals to those who work for him that he expects them to have zero tolerance too.

WHAT DO ETITICAL LEADERS DO?

Ethical leaders have a number of characteristics that make them ethical. Ironically, they often don't realize they have these characteristics. Nor do they realize the power of role-modelling them clearly, and rewarding others who also role-model ethical behaviour. A good first step to maintaining an ethical organizational culture is to make sure the boss is consciously aware of what he or she does to set the right culture. In this section we take a look at the characteristics of ethical leaders, some of them are certainly antithetical to the notion of strong leadership that we have been fed by the media in recent years.

Think of bosses you have known who have true integrity and you would label as ethical leaders. As Jim Collins observed, they are the ones who put the greater good before their own ego. They are the ones you don't hear boasting about themselves and their successes. Why? Because they are less concerned with inflating their own ego and more concerned about the greater good and doing something worthwhile.

Ethical leadership is not about being perfect but is about constantly striving to do the right thing, candour and diligently correcting wrongdoings and keeping organizations on the right track. Leaders who do this are not limelight seekers; they are the ones who quietly and determinedly work to guide their people through challenges and dilemmas. They don't act in a knee-jerk fashion, they know which issues need careful consideration and they give time to those issues. They consider the people as well as the organizational implications of decisions and always treat people with humanity and respect. They have clear goals but pay attention to how the goal is achieved as well as to what is achieved so that ethics is not compromised.

Joseph Badaracco[4] makes the point: 'The vast majority of difficult, important human problems – both inside and outside organizations – are not solved by a swift, decisive stroke from someone at the top. What usually matters are careful, thoughtful, small, practical efforts by people working far from the limelight.'

The leader also needs to have foresight and experience. This is where role models and mentors come in. They have the experience to understand how situations can play out if they are not handled well. A former CEO, John, who is now a mentor of business leaders told me that he is astonished at how many of the people that he mentors encounter ethical issues but simply do not identify them as such. He said that he believed that this is due to lack of experience, lack of integrity, the unwillingness to tackle difficult situations or a combination of all three.

John is a wise and confident man in his sixties and is not concerned about what his mentees think about his advice. He believes that his job is to tell them what they need to hear. This happens less frequently in the workplace because people are conscious of their place in the hierarchy and often do not challenge those above them. That is unless it is known that the leader absolutely expects it.

The best leaders expect the highest moral standards of people. They create an environment where people speak up, tell the truth (unpalatable as it may be at times), take accountability and put the organization's needs before their own. They insist on these standards of behaviour from everyone in the organization, with no exceptions. They also appreciate that ethical challenges may not be recognized as such by inexperienced managers so they make it clear that they expect anyone who is in any way concerned about a situation to seek advice from a more experienced colleague.

The following are essential characteristics of an ethical leader. The CEO needs to articulate and insist upon these characteristics. And the ways that they insist upon them is by role-modelling them themselves, by 'rewarding' those who do the same and 'punishing' those who don't.

Experience

However, as John pointed out to me it is not enough just to have role models. It is important to have the experience to be able to identify when a situation is an ethical one and to know how to approach it. The leader of an organization needs to make sure that people like John are available to mentor and coach others.

It doesn't matter whether they work for the organization or are external mentors. What matters is that managers know they are there and know that they are expected to consult them if they are in any way concerned about something that has happened and are not sure what to do.

Transparency

The usual definition of the word 'transparency' in the business context is to do with full disclosure of financial information to investors. However, it is about much more than compliance and regulation. It is about the free flow of information and knowledge around the organization. Access to the right information when people need it is necessary if people are to do a good job. It is also necessary to create a culture where nothing is hidden or out of bounds. True transparency can only occur in a high-trust culture. Bosses need to trust employees with data that they wouldn't want to get into the hands of competitors, for example.

Managers sometimes associate the holding of information as a privilege of their position. Along with the status of a management job comes the power of being given information that others are not privy to. They only reveal it to others on a 'need to know' basis.

The over-thirties are used to a working world where their employers had the power because they could control how much and what information was released to the workers. Information can no longer be restricted nor its release controlled in the same way as it could before the ubiquity of the Internet. Generation Y (those born after 1980) cannot understand the world of work where those at the top of the hierarchy have more access to information than anyone else. It doesn't make sense to them and it is indeed a legacy of bygone days that deserves to die. Organizations still act as if they have control over their information but of course they don't in the same way that they used to. It is a question of trust. The restricting of information as well as restricting use of websites such as Facebook is all about a lack of trust in employees to do the right thing. Often organizational leaders underestimate the effects of their actions when they take decisions that are tantamount to telling employees 'we don't trust you'.

Consciousness

As a leader a raised level of consciousness of the reasons for and effects of your actions will set you apart from the rest – and is in fact essential to truly ethical leadership.

Most of us act automatically, instinctively and 'unconsciously' most of the time. The older we get, the more that the situations we encounter are repeats, or appear to be repeats. Therefore we keep repeating the same courses of action without really thinking too deeply about why we are doing what we are doing. Often we are not even consciously aware of the values, beliefs and assumptions that underpin our actions and decisions. This is risky when it comes to dealing with matters of ethical concern where we may be called upon to explain our rationale for a particular course of action.

An example was the case of an HR manager in a large blue-chip organization who was grilled by the CEO about the performance rating system that the company used. It was a forced distribution model that required managers to rate a certain percentage of their people as performing poorly, a certain percentage as performing exceptionally, etc. for performance appraisal. This practice gained in popularity on the endorsement of Jack Welch when he was CEO of General Electric. The CEO had heard complaints about the system and wanted to know the rationale behind it. He quoted the management writer Ed Lawler's criticism of the approach: '... it is a bureaucratic solution to a serious leadership failure'.

The HR manager was flummoxed. The only defence that he could offer was that most big organizations use it and it is a way of keeping pay increases from spiralling out of control.

The truth was that he had accepted the system without question. He hadn't questioned its efficacy even though he knew that people thought it grossly unfair. If he had sought to understand the underlying reasons behind the forced distribution system he would have realized that the best solution was to address the deficiencies in management not to continue with this system. He would also not have blindly assumed it was acceptable because lots of other organizations do it. As the CEO pointed out, so many organizations use the system because they shy away from addressing the real issue which is ineffective leadership.

This is just one example of how managers can blindly go about their work and inadvertently perpetuate problems. Questioning long-time practices and sacred cows is the job of a manager. The job of a CEO is to get the message across that this is what he expects managers to do.

There is another issue relating to consciousness that is key to managers' ability to make ethical decisions. It is the issue of unconscious bias. Most organizations in their quest to become fair and equitable have policies relating to fair treatment of people irrespective of their race, age, gender, sexual orientation and so on. The problem is, most of us believe that we are unbiased and objective in our treatment of others. However, the research tells us that we are wrong in this assumption about ourselves. David Armor, professor of psychology at Yale University, has researched the tendency of people to believe that they are free from biases which they are quick to recognize in others. He calls it 'the illusion of objectivity'. Basically his findings show that most people are influenced by unconscious thoughts and decisions yet believe that they are making objective and unbiased decisions. They hold implicit prejudices that are based upon humans' unconscious tendency to make associations. Someone may be free from any conscious forms of prejudice such as racism but may harbour a bias that is, for example, based upon associating black men and violence.

Tony Greenwald, a professor of psychology at the University of Washington, devised a test called the Implicit Association Test (IAT). He used the test to study unconscious bias. At the time of writing, more than 2.5 million tests have been taken by people all over the world. The test takers have to make split-second good/bad distinctions between words like 'love', 'pain', 'sorrow' and at the same time sort images of faces that are young/old, black/white, etc. depending on what bias is being tested for. It works by detecting subtle changes in reaction time. People who believe that they have no conscious bias towards, say, old people are slower to associate the word 'old' with 'good' words than they are to associate the word 'young' with 'good' words. It is believed to be a good indicator of bias because it is assessing the automatic response of people. If a person takes too long to respond the test is invalid.

The implications of unconscious biases are clear. Good people may be deselected from jobs because the interviewer holds a bias that they are not even aware of. The risks to the organization stretch beyond missing out on the best talent, they also include the possibility of legal cases that can cost organizations money as well as their reputation. Courts can and do use implicit biases as the bases for rulings. One example of this was *Thomas vs Kodak* in the USA in 1999 where the court ruled that race discrimination had occurred and stated that 'prohibition against "disparate treatment because of race" extends both to employer acts based on conscious racial animus and to employer decisions that are based on stereotyped thinking or other forms of less conscious bias.'

By its very nature, unconscious bias is very difficult for leaders and organizations to overcome. The first step is to ensure that managers understand that we all have unconscious biases so that they can start to become mindful of their own by, for example, doing the online IAT test. That way they can be alerted to their unconscious biases and therefore become vigilant so that they have a chance of guarding against them.

Candour

Candour is the quality of being truthful, straightforward and honest. It is not just about telling the truth, it is about telling the whole truth. Some people are adept at telling the truth while omitting information knowing they are giving an impression of something while meaning something else. This is selective truth telling, it is not candour. For example, I once asked an employee who was based in New York whether he was happy in his work (I had concerns and wanted to find out whether there was anything wrong). His answer was 'there is nowhere else I would rather be'. It transpired that he was telling me the truth but he was withholding information. What he actually meant was there was nowhere else he would rather be than in New York but he was planning to quit his job as he was not at all happy in it. He wanted to give me the impression that he was happy in his job though because he was not yet ready to move.

Con-men use this approach too. They are adept of appearing honest and truthful and are very skilled at getting people to trust them. Business leaders and politicians have been shown to be capable of that too. PR at its worst gives the impression of something that is not wholly true but does so without telling lies.

The corporate scandals of the 1990s and 2000s have shown that not all of those in positions of power are honest. The only way a leader can prove their honesty is by displaying candour. One of the best opportunities to do that is when they or someone else has made a mistake and they take the opportunity to state the whole truth about a situation.

Taking responsibility

Finally, and very obviously, leaders need to take personal responsibility for making sure that their organization is ethical. This includes making it clear to senior management and all employees what standards are required and that no transgressions will be overlooked. This can be trickier than it sounds because it means that even if your best sales person does something out of line you will not 'let it go' just because they are big revenue earners. Often ethical standards become flexible as soon as revenue is at stake. One company had a very clear policy of not speculating with currency. This policy was well known. However, a senior person saw an opportunity one day and gambled with several hundred thousand dollars. The gamble paid off and he made a lot of money for the company. The senior management team felt that they had a dilemma. This employee had brought in a huge sum of money yet he had knowingly broken a golden rule of the company. Should they congratulate him or sack him? Had he lost a lot of money in the deal the decision would have been clear. I don't know what the outcome of this case was but the point is that this is a time when an organization needs to decide whether the short-term gain, i.e. keeping the person, is more important than the long term view, i.e. running a business ethically.

So, thinking back to the moral philosophies in Chapter 3, the management were concerned with whether the consequences of an action (utilitarianism), i.e. the most good for the largest number of people, made it right. But the question for this senior management group was whether the ends justify the means. Following the categorical moral principles approach they would come to the conclusion that the ends do not justify the means. If they were to let this incident go, the signal sent to others in the organization would be that you can go against company policy and will not be punished providing that there are no negative consequences.

This sort of occurrence really does test the ethical mettle of the leader. Few would fire someone in this situation. Some would probably discipline him but most would probably let it go and hope that the word didn't spread too widely.

The real question for the leader is what kind of organiza-tion does he want to preside over? James Burke was CEO of

Johnson and Johnson in 1982 when their product Tylenol was tampered with and seven people died of cyanide poisoning. His behaviour meant that Johnson and Johnson were, and still are nearly 30 years later, used as an example of a beacon of trust and high ethical standards. Sure, Johnson and Johnson have their famous credo that outlines its code of conduct but it was the strong moral character and actions of James Burke that meant that the company not only survived this terrible crisis but actually enhanced its reputation enormously. Burke not only withdrew 31 million bottles of Tylenol, he launched a big communications campaign to inform and reassure the public, he allowed the media into strategy sessions and introduced tamper-resistant packaging. James Burke had no choice but to take responsibility in this crisis. He really did demonstrate that he believed his responsibility was not only to remove immediate risk but to regain the customers' trust by doing more than was necessary or might have been expected. His actions together with his calm and assured manner have earned the company a reputation that is of course one of its biggest assets.

DEVELOPING ETHICAL LEADERS

As we have seen, our moral code and values are developed in childhood. This early conditioning is far from easy to change. It is debatable whether organizations should even try to change it.

And certainly it is unlikely that leaders will change much once they have reached the top level in an organization. The only time that tends to happen is when a person has experienced a trauma which changes them in some fundamental way.

So how do you develop ethical leaders?

A dominant theme in the literature on leadership is that it can and must be taught. When it comes to ethical leadership, more than 60% of respondents in the 'Ethics in the Workplace' Survey said that training managers how to handle ethical issues is important but only around 20% said that their organizations did not have training for managers.

However, ethical leadership cannot be *taught*; it must be *learnt*. The nature of ethical issues means that in order to be competent at handling them a person must grapple with and reflect upon them. So the process is more of a discovery process than one of being fed certain essential information that can be followed by rote. This is perhaps true of many subjects; we have long known that the person in the classroom who learns the most is the teacher. This is a significant point. It means that 'training' programmes need to be designed as learning experiences. The tendency is to deliver materials and provide teaching not learning. Ethics is a subject that requires people to explore and grapple with their own views in order to appreciate what it takes to run an ethical organization. To be effective it has to be designed as an inquiry-based learning event.

Guidance from mentors who can help the mentees to learn from their experience is also really important in developing ethical leaders.

ETHICAL LEADERSHIP DEVELOPMENT PROGRAMME

Creating an effective ethical leadership development programme

If you are committed to developing an ethical organizational culture you have to have an ethical leadership programme.

Ethical leadership is a core discipline of management these days. It is as important as finance and so shouldn't be left to chance. A CEO who is committed to ensuring that the organization is ethical understands that it is a complex subject. He or she is prepared to spend the money to ensure that those who are leading others have the knowledge and practical tools they need to run their business ethically.

The question is where do you start? The tendency and temptation is to start by issuing a code of conduct that has been developed centrally. A better place to start is to engage the organization's leaders in a conversation about ethics and have them contribute their thinking. This approach ensures that they learn much more and are better equipped to impart their knowledge and thinking to others. It also means that they are likely to support the code of ethics specifically and create an ethically organizational culture generally, rather than feel that it is imposed upon them. This conversation should take place within an ethical leadership programme.

Key principles and core components of the programme

There are a few principles that will help to ensure that an ethical leadership programme is a success:

- *An exploration of personal morality.*   This has to be at the heart of any ethical leadership programme. Ethics is by its very nature personal. The decisions that leaders make are to some extent governed by their own personal moral values. Many people are not clear about what their own values are simply because they haven't had reason to think about it before. Providing the opportunity and environment to explore personal values and morality is important at the beginning of the programme.

- *Learning through conversation.*   Facilitated conversations should be at the heart of the programme – it cannot be emphasized enough that people learn more if they discover for themselves rather than being 'taught'. Ethics is a complex subject and so people need to be able to grapple with it rather than be spoon fed. Better that they grapple in the safe confines of a programme than flounder when an ethical issue arises in real life!

  There should be very little 'lecturing' other than to introduce the moral philosophies and the decision-making framework (in Chapter 1). Topics of conversation should include the nature of ethics, the relevance of ethics to contemporary business and workplaces, personal morality, leadership responsibility for ethics, moral philosophy and case studies.

- *Involvement.*   Leaders are much more likely to take responsibility for developing and maintaining an ethical culture if they are involved in establishing the need for it and understand the nature of the challenge. Having them discover rather than teaching them is much more likely to make them feel involved and ultimately committed.

- *Mandatory.*   The programme should be mandatory. This is an obvious point but if it is not mandatory the signal that is sent is that it is not important. Some managers and leaders may already have taken ethics courses at business school but it is important that they do the course within their own context and with their own colleagues.
- *Creation of mentors.*   An explicit goal of a learning programme should be for those who attend to decide if they are sufficiently interested to volunteer to become mentors. See the section below on developing mentors.

The content. An ethical leadership programme should cover the following:

- The nature of ethics
- The nature of business and the place of ethics in business
- Personal values and morality
- The major ethical philosophies and their practical relevance in business and organizational life
- The leader's role, accountability and role modelling

- Standards of behaviour (and contents of the code of conduct if relevant)
- The decision-making framework
- Exercises – tackling ethical dilemmas using the knowledge and insight they have acquired and the decision-making framework
- Challenging wrongdoings and why we don't (the four excuses)
- The skills of having a difficult conversation
- Mentoring skills

I have covered all of these topics except the last three in the preceding chapters. See below to read more about mentoring. As for the ability to challenge wrongdoings and the skills of having a difficult conversation, these are a crucial part of handling ethical issues so I will cover them in some detail here.

Challenging wrongdoings.   Courage is an underestimated trait of great people and great managers. And it is a trait that is needed when dealing with ethical issues.

Many a person has stayed silent when they have noticed something happening that is not right. And there are reasons we give ourselves for not speaking up. One that I hear sometimes from fellow consultants is that the client is the client and they are always right. This comment reveals the fact that when we are in a relationship where we perceive that the other person has more power than us we can do things that we know are wrong. The client has more power than you because they can decide not to hire you again if you don't do what they want you to do. Your boss has more power because he or she can fire you. It is understandable that people might compromise their ethics in order to make a living. However, there is a price to pay for an organization and for all individuals concerned when this happens. And silence – while it may be the response of a pragmatic person it is not the response of a courageous one. Conversations on ethical development programmes for managers need to be had about these kinds of issues as they represent the real challenges that managers have to face in their organizational lives.

Mary C. Gentile, a senior research scholar at Babson College, Wellesley, Massachusetts, has identified four reasons why managers stay silent in the face of an ethical situation: 'It's standard practice', 'It's not a big deal', 'I want to be loyal' and 'It's not my responsibility'. These are rationalizations that are common and sometimes when people use them they genuinely do believe their own rationale. Other times, deep down they don't but it is easier to have an excuse not to deal with the situation than to face up to a difficult challenge.

I recently heard a good example of an 'it's standard practice' rationalization in relation to the use of materials without seeking copyright permission. Two people were in disagreement, one wanted to photocopy some articles to send to a client and the other was saying that they needed to seek permission from the owner of the copyright first. The person who wanted to make the copies said 'everybody does it'. This kind of rationalization is not uncommon and some would argue that it is not serious. The dangerous part of this is the easy way in which people can end up doing things that are unethical (and indeed sometimes illegal as in this example). Often it happens without the person thinking too much about it. The problem is that this kind of behaviour can become the norm in an organization so that before you know it all sorts of unethical practices are happening under the guise of 'it's standard practice'. It can be hard for people to challenge others in these circumstances because the challenger can be accused of being rather righteous, overly rule-following and inflexible which can make them easily back down.

'It's not a big deal' is another commonly used reason why ethical behaviour can go unchecked. An example may be stealing company stationery. It happens a lot and people probably think it's a perk of the job and what does it matter if people take a few paperclips now and then? This kind of issue can be brushed off without too much thought which in itself is a risky approach as it means that underlying problems are not uncovered. One of the problems that was identified from the 2010 Ethics in the Workplace research was managers not recognizing something as an ethical issue in the first place. The 'no big deal' response is often an off-the-cuff one that people make without stopping and thinking. The danger is that whatever it is that is being labelled as no big deal could be one of those ethical issues that has not been identified as such.

One of the particularly tough challenges for people in organizations is a conflict between being loyal and wanting to do the right thing. It is not that loyalty isn't a genuine cause of an ethical dilemma, but it is sometimes used as an excuse. An example of such a situation is where a sales person sees an opportunity to sell something to a client but the best thing for that client is to actually buy a product from a different business unit. This means that the client will get what is best for them but the sales revenue and commission will go to another sales team. The sales person's dilemma is that on the one hand he wants to do the right thing for the client, but on the other he feels deep loyalty towards her colleagues. When it would have been just as easy to sell something from his own business unit this represents a real test. And the 'I want to be loyal to my team' excuse for keeping the business would be an obvious one to make.

'It's not my responsibility' is a common excuse or rationale for doing nothing. It is used when people see something wrong in a different department, or that they think the CEO should be dealing with or that they could say they do not have the authority necessary to deal with it.

Organizational culture and role modelling by leaders are the factors that set a context where these excuses are less used because they are not acceptable. Any ethics training of managers and employees needs to include a session on these excuses. They are common, it is easy, and sometimes human nature to want to use them. Getting them out in the open as a topic of conversation is essential.

The skills of having a difficult conversation.   Whether it is to do with performance improvement, disciplinary matters or ethical issues, most people don't relish the thought of having a difficult conversation. In my years of working with managers in many organizations I haven't met one person who enjoys this part of the job. Mostly I have found that people are nervous about it because of one or more of the following reasons: they lack confidence that they will do it well; they are afraid of the other person's reaction; they hate the fact that they cannot predict how the employee will take it; they are worried that the person will become angry or upset; they hate to be the 'bad' guy. They may also be worried about being labelled as too much of a stickler, self-righteous or rigid.

In my survey 'Ethics in the Workplace' nearly 20% of respondents reported that one of the challenges that they had encountered when dealing with ethical situations was that they were worried about tackling the situation.

To some extent it is human nature to want to avoid these kinds of confrontations. However, there is no getting away from the fact that if you are dealing with an ethical issue it is inevitable that you will have to have a difficult conversation. Or, as I prefer to think about it, a 'courageous' conversation. This is an important component of training for managers to enable them to get to grips with the skills inherent in handling a difficult conversation as well as the confidence to do it.

The key skills and attitudes needed to handle such a conversation are the ability to build rapport, to see such conversations as a key part of your responsibility, to depersonalize it, to approach the conversation in a spirit of inquiry and therefore ask good questions, to challenge rationalizations, to enable those involved to see the long-term risks and consequences as well the short-term imperatives and to generate viable alternatives with those with whom you are having the conversation.

The questioning framework is a useful tool to use in difficult conversations because it keeps the focus on the issue which helps to keep it professional and focused and not emotional.

The capabilities outlined above are straightforward and probably quite obvious, except perhaps for building rapport.

This is a much misunderstood and underused tool. People usually think of rapport as a harmonious state of agreement. It *is* about harmony but is to do with people understanding and appreciating one another's points of view and feelings. So you can actually be in disagreement with someone and still stay in rapport with them. In fact that is the only way to be if you are to reach resolution. Maintaining rapport during a difficult conversation is the most valuable tool you have. In practice it means genuinely listening to the person and showing you are listening – saying things like 'I can see why you are saying that'. It also means using the language of agreement. So while you may not agree with the content of what they are saying or proposing to do, you can agree with their intentions or feelings – 'that's right, you are worried about being disloyal'. If you stay in rapport with someone it makes challenging them and their actions much easier.

Mentoring

A culture of mentoring is a great asset when it comes to creating an ethical business. Having skilled managers and employees who don't think twice about seeking input from a mentor means that potential ethical problems can be identified and resolved quickly. As already noted, often ethical problems arise because managers are not experienced enough to identify when an issue has the potential to turn into an ethical problem. An experienced mentor has the experience to notice the alarm bells when they start ringing and to appreciate the possible consequences of the situation.

The 'Ethics in the Workplace' research showed that over 30% of respondents from the not-for-profit sectors said it was important for organizations to offer mentoring; almost 50% of people from the private sector and more than 50% from the public sector said the same. However, in all sectors fewer than 20% of respondents said that their organization used mentoring.

The lack of mentors and mentoring programmes could be explained because they tend to have a bad reputation in companies as they often don't create any value or motivation for those involved. This is often due to a few factors: unskilled mentors who do not know how to have a good mentoring conversation, unwilling mentees who are not sure what they can get from being mentored and what I call 'mentoring in a vacuum', that is having nothing specific to talk about. All of these problems can easily be fixed by following a few key principles when setting up a mentoring programme.

Key principles of a good mentoring programme

- Mentors must want to be mentors – to do it well a mentor must really want to do it. Don't nominate people to be mentors, ask for volunteers.
- Select mentors who have the right strengths: a passion for helping people to learn, good listening skills, the ability to

encourage and have a high-support high-challenge conversation, and to be motivated by the other succeeding.

- Train mentors and mentees together so that they explore the expectations they have of one another and they learn and practice the skills of high-support high-challenge conversations.
- Ensure that the mentors have the time to fulfil the role and can be available to help. A manager who never has room in his schedule is not worth training.
- Train the mentors to have 'ethical dilemma' conversations and train them in the use of the questioning framework.
- The programme must cover confidentiality. There will be times when a mentor cannot keep the situation confidential and he or she needs to know how to handle that with the mentee.

Ethical mentoring is unlike the usual form of mentoring where people meet regularly. Therefore it is important that everyone in the organization knows who the mentors are and feels able to approach them if they are concerned about something.

In order that the mentors have the knowledge, skills and practice that they will need to fulfil the role, it is a good idea if they are also responsible for running ethical practice workshops in the organization. Having to teach people is the best way to learn a subject yourself. Also, running the workshops will give the mentors a good idea of the kinds of issues that people are concerned about and dealing with and will thus build their own knowledge and understanding.

There are many benefits of having a cadre of known ethical mentors. However, there is also a danger. The danger is that managers who are not mentors shirk their responsibility to create an ethical context. It must be made clear to all managers that ethics is seen as a core management discipline and as such they are expected to be knowledgeable and competent.

In this chapter we have looked at ethical leadership and the characteristics of an ethical leader. We have also looked at the influence of ethical leadership and the power it has to ensure that an organization is ethical, or not. Even those who have high moral standards sometimes struggle to handle ethical issues so it is essential that organizations protect themselves and their people by providing structured training for their leaders. This chapter provided you with guidance on what an ethical leadership programme and a mentoring programme need to cover. You can use this book as a handbook for the programme.

CHAPTER 5

Ethical Working Cultures

What this chapter will do for you.
You will learn:

- What is meant by 'organizational culture'
- Why it is important to have an ethical culture
- The characteristics of an ethical organizational culture
- The challenges of creating an ethical culture
- The essentials of creating an ethical culture

WHAT IS ORGANIZATIONAL CULTURE?

As we have already seen, context is a key determinant of people's behaviour. This means that the culture of the organization has to reward ethical behaviour and punish unethical behaviour.

But what exactly do we mean by 'culture'? The culture is the environmental conditions that affect the different parts of the organization. The professor, researcher and writer Edgar Schein defines culture as follows:

A pattern of shared basic assumptions that the group learned as it solved its problems of external adaptation and internal integration, that has worked well enough to be considered valid and therefore, to be taught to new members as the correct way to perceive, think, and feel in relation to those problems.

The culture of an organization is made up of a number of elements:

- The commonly held stated and unstated values
- Implicit and explicit expectations about the behaviour of its employees
- Customs and rituals
- Stories and myths about the history of the organization and its members
- Commonly used language
- The physical space
- Metaphors and symbols that are an intrinsic part of the organization and how it works

New employees tend to learn about the organizational culture by experiencing it. They may be told that certain kinds of behaviour are expected but more often than not they learn about the culture as they go along. Employees may struggle to articulate their organization's culture but they usually know what is acceptable and what is not acceptable. Often the espoused culture is different from the actual culture. For example, new employees may be told that it is acceptable to say what they think and speak their mind but find that when they do so others do not respond well. They are not necessarily being deliberately misled; rather the culture is being described as people would like it to be, not as it actually is. This is not necessarily a deliberate attempt to deceive but a mild form of delusion or wishing things were different. It is often the case that we are unconscious of the culture within which we dwell. It is certainly true of country cultures – it takes an outsider to really see them for what they are.

In order to fit into any particular culture people emulate the behaviour of those already in the culture. They particularly take their lead from those in charge. Therefore leaders play a very large role in setting the prevailing culture of an organization. In order that employees really understand what is expected and not expected, leaders need to convey how they want people to behave in actions as well as words.

WHY IS IT IMPORTANT TO HAVE AN ETHICAL CULTURE?

In the 'Ethics in the Workplace' Survey 70% of respondents said that they believed it was important to have an ethical culture. Organizational culture is a powerful but informal regulator of behaviour. Without this regulation employees may intentionally or unintentionally do things that could get them or the organization into trouble. Some organizations have formal codes of conduct. These are useful in setting boundaries of behaviour but organizational culture is far more influential than any code of conduct.

THE CHARACTERISTICS OF AN ETHICAL CULTURE

Many organizations try to build ethical cultures by putting the emphasis on compliance and introducing procedures, rules, regulations, an independent board and codes of conduct. It is easier to introduce new regulations and processes than it is to change culture. This explains why so many organizations favour introducing process rather than tackling the messy and difficult business of culture change.

Processes and systems do not create an ethical culture. At best they create a culture of compliance. At worst they make it harder to achieve an ethical culture. The reason is that managers breathe a sigh of relief that everything is all right – the rules are in place and everyone knows them. They do not take account of the fact that people can find ways around rules if they want to, that no amount of rules can account for every possible eventuality. And that it is not the rules but the context that largely drives behaviour.

In order to create an ethical culture you have to look at the whole system. Compliance is an important part of the system as it provides guidance and standards. But it is just one part of the system. As we have seen in recent years, organizations with great compliance procedures, such as investment banks, are not necessarily the most ethical. Culture trumps procedures every time.

There are a number of aspects of an organization's culture and competence that determine its ethics: leadership, a focus on doing the right thing, a sense of purpose, a sense of responsibility, engagement, hiring the right people, managers role-modelling the right behaviour, knowledge and skills, a 'learning' mindset and a code of conduct.

We have already looked at leadership in Chapter 4. As we have seen, an organization can never be ethical unless the people who run it role-model ethical behaviour and set the standards. But ethical leadership is not enough on its own. An organization is a system and each part of the system cannot be treated as a separate part that is disconnected from the other parts. Each part affects the other parts. This is an important concept to grasp in order to understand how ethical cultures are created. For example, take one part of a system – a code of conduct. This is a good thing to have in itself but the other parts of the organization that affect it and are affected by it have to be in synch. For example, the performance management procedures have to reinforce the code of conduct as does the leaders' behaviour. The Johnson and Johnson Tylenol case illustrates this. J&J had a 'credo' that governed their behaviour. The CEO followed the credo to the letter in his actions following the death of the people who had taken Tylenol capsules which had been tampered with. If he had not, then every person in his organization as well as every partner would have received a clear but unspoken message that profits come before patients. In other words, that the credo was a part of the system that could be ignored if the boss chose to ignore it. Messages about ethics must be consistent in word and deed, and all parts of the organization must support the core message.

Doing the right thing

One of the common problems that prevent organizations from being as ethical as they could be is the tendency of managers to do things right rather than doing the right thing. The late Professor Russell Ackoff, organizational systems theorist and consultant, talked about 'doing the wrong thing righter'. He noted that the more right you do the wrong thing the more wrong it becomes. An example might be a performance management system that is flawed because it does not require people to learn from mistakes. The right thing to do might be to reward people for their ability to learn not to do only what they believe they can get right first time. The more perfect the performance management system becomes at measuring the wrong thing, the more wrong it becomes.

A culture of ethics rewards people for doing the right thing and for challenging the wrong things. Part of that is a tolerance for mistakes, provided that those mistakes are learned from and not covered up for fear of 'punishment'. One company gives an annual award for the best mistake made last year – it is the mistake from which the corporation learned most.

August Busch of Anheuser Busch once put up a poster saying something like 'If you didn't make a serious mistake last year you didn't do your job. But if you make the same mistake twice you won't be here next year'. The company had a tolerance for mistakes but not for not learning. An organization with an ethical culture has a mindset of wanting to get things right – part and parcel of that is a desire to learn in order to do the right thing.

A sense of purpose

It is not always easy to know the right thing to do. A clear sense of purpose is essential. What are you here to do? Back to the performance management example above, if your purpose is to innovate and create new products that consumers will want to buy then you need to try new things. It is impossible to get it right all the time so you need people to be prepared to fail sometimes and to learn from their failures. Knowing that your purpose is innovation helps people to decide what the right thing to do is at any one time.

Harvard Business School professor Michael Beer researched the difference between companies that achieve high performance levels over long time periods and those that fail when they reach a certain size. He analysed the companies that failed in the 2009 financial crash and suggested three core reasons;

the companies lacked a higher purpose (they were focused on short-term gains not long-term value), they did not have a clear strategy and they badly mismanaged risk.

In contrast, two companies, Charles Schwab and US Bancorp, survived the crisis because they had a strong focus on customer service and on honesty and transparency. Neither company did business in the subprime market because they did not believe it was the kind of business that was sustainable in the long term.

Responsibility

For an ethical culture to prevail, employees also need to feel responsible and accountable for their actions. In the 'Ethics in the Workplace' Survey, 70% of respondents believed that it is important that employees feel responsible for and committed to ethical practice. However around 40% believed that employees in their organizations did feel that way.

Ethical transgressions are always a result of a person or group of people doing something wrong. Without a sense of personal accountability people can blame their boss or the organization. They need to have an internal locus of control, in other words, a belief that they are responsible for and can largely influence what happens. People with an external locus of control mostly believe that they have little or no control over what happens to them. They hand over responsibility to other people or to 'the system' and have a sense of helplessness over their ability to influence and control anything. This does not mean that they are any less ethical than people with an internal locus of control. It means that they believe that they cannot influence outcomes. Those with an internal locus of control believe that they can influence outcomes which is good provided that their intentions are ethical. The ideal scenario is to have people who have positive intent who want to take responsibility and who believe that they can influence outcomes. Creating an environment where people are expected to stand up for what they believe is right and take responsibility is crucial. Without it there can be no ethical culture as small and large daily wrongdoings will go unchecked. It is the regular employees who know what is going on. Bad things are hidden from management so organizations need to create a strong culture of speaking up and standing up for what is right.

However, you cannot give people responsibility for something without giving them the knowledge and skills they need to exercise their responsibility.

EMPLOYEES' WORKSHOPS

Running workshops for employees has two specific benefits. It is a great way of involving them in establishing standards of behaviour and it helps to educate them about ethical issues. A workshop format is also a great way of getting engagement and buy-in to the organization's code of conduct. This is covered in more detail in the 'code of conduct' section below. The key areas that should be covered in an employee workshop are as follows.

An exploration of personal morality

As we have already seen, personal morality has to be at the heart of any discussion on ethics. Ethics workshops tend only to be run for leaders and even when they are run for employees they tend to focus on telling them what the standards of behaviour are. Agreeing standards of behaviour and getting buy-in to your code of conduct are of course crucial. But ethical dilemmas, by their nature, are not about following rules and standards; they are about making often difficult judgements based upon our personal moral values. Anyone can encounter moral issues, so it is in organizations' interests to prepare their people as much as possible to handle them.

Introduction to the key moral philosophies and decision-making framework

Understanding the basics of the utilitarian, deontology and virtue ethics philosophies is important as it raises people's awareness of the different ways of looking at situations. The use of examples for the group to discuss helps them to be able to identify a potential ethical dilemma in the first place. Applying the decision-making framework gives employees practice in handling ethical situations as well as increasing their knowledge of the issues surrounding ethics. Just as with leaders, a discovery-based approach to learning is far more effective than a 'tell' or 'teaching' approach. It is also very powerful to have the employees discuss real ethical issues that they have encountered themselves. It is an excellent way of making the subject relevant and useful to them.

Discussion about responsibilities

It may be that you have a code of conduct or something similar that indicates the responsibilities that the organization bestows upon its various members. Whether or not you do formally lay out responsibilities in this way, it is a missed opportunity not to get employees to think through for themselves what they believe their responsibilities are. Workshop facilitators are sometimes nervous of opening up the conversation in this way in case the participants don't come up with the 'right' answers. In my experience once people have discussed their own experience of ethical dilemmas from their own lives they can clearly see what their responsibilities are to themselves, their colleagues and their organization.

Where to go for help

Inevitably people will feel some degree of concern that they are able to properly identify and handle ethical issues at work. It is therefore important to talk about the support and advice that is available to them in the form of their managers, mentors and possibly even an ethics helpline if you have one in place.

Dealing with fear and excuses

It can take a great deal of courage to challenge the behaviour of others, especially bosses, or to raise concerns about established company practices. As we saw in the previous chapter, there can also be a temptation to shy away from dealing with tricky ethical issues and come up with excuses. Fear is probably the most common reason that unethical practices are allowed to continue. This is a very real issue and must be tackled in the workshop setting. If it is not, no amount of awareness of the issues will make any difference. Remember the case of Paul Moore, the whistleblower from HBOS bank? He had good reason to be worried about repercussions on him if he continued to challenge aspects of the sales practices that he believed to be putting the bank at risk. Having heard him being interviewed it seemed clear that it took a lot of courage to blow the whistle.

After the workshop

It is important that the workshop is not the last people hear about ethics. An ethical culture is one where they are encouraged to raise issues of concern. It is no good for people to learn about ethics on the workshop if they are nervous of challenging something they believe to be unethical or are afraid of asking for help. Managers and mentors need to be available and approachable.

As we have seen, ethical issues are some of the most challenging people have to deal with. Providing them with practical tools as well as a sound understanding of the issues is essential. Relying on them to use their own judgement and find their own way of approaching these issues is exposing your organization to unnecessary risk. It is also missing an opportunity to signal that ethics and creating an ethical culture is a priority.

Engagement

People who have an internal locus of control and a shared sense of purpose with their organization and colleagues tend to be highly engaged. Those who don't have a strong internal sense of what is right don't tend to stick their neck out and argue for the right thing.

Organizations spend a great deal of time and money trying to understand what engages their people and attempting to raise engagement levels. Most large organizations employ someone who is responsible for employee engagement. This is laudable. However, they often miss the point – engagement mostly comes from inside someone, rather than from external stimuli. By definition, engagement means being energized and committed to doing something. This happens when the person truly believes that it's the right thing to do and/or has some intrinsic motivation to do it. Companies rarely take time to discover people's intrinsic motivations. When it comes to hiring ethical people though, this is essential. A common mistake is to hire people with 'passion' in the hope that this passion will mean that the person will be determined to do a great job. But they also need to be intrinsically motivated to do something that benefits either a cause or people other than themselves. It is important to hire people who want to do the right thing for all concerned. If that is missing they can and do become tempted to cut corners to achieve what they want. They need to want to do the right thing as distinct from just doing things right.

An example of this was a small organization set up by a group of friends who were copywriters. Their purpose was to offer copywriting services to businesses. They had all worked in the corporate world and had set up their business partly because they wanted to work to their own standards and values. One of the values they had was not to work with organizations that knowingly did harm to consumers. This clearly ruled out tobacco companies. They all agreed to this. However, one day one of them received a phone call from a friend whose relative was a senior person in marketing in a big tobacco firm. He was offering the opportunity to pitch for a piece of business worth around £50,000. This would have been by far the biggest project in revenue terms that the group would have won. Bob, the partner who took the call, knew that working with this company was against the agreed principles of the group and so decided not to consult with them but to pitch for it anyway. This resulted in a major disagreement. The other partners' view was that no amount of money would entice them to work with a tobacco company. They said their conscience would not permit it. Bob, on the other hand, was very driven by money. He admitted that he would work for just about anyone if it meant financial gain for him personally. In this case Bob's business partners learned the hard way about working with others whose values are different from their own. It can be very tough to check these things out when hiring someone. The best way is to pose scenarios to them and ask how they would handle them.

Hiring the right people

It is much easier to hire people who have high moral standards than to try to change those who haven't. Checking out people's ethics at the point of hiring is crucially important. This means asking them specific questions about ethical dilemmas they have encountered and how they have handled them as well as questioning them on hypothetical situations. You can normally get a good sense of someone's moral character by doing this. Ethical people understand that it is not always easy to know what the right thing to do is. Look for evidence of them struggling to figure out the right thing. People who are either faking high morals or who have little experience to draw upon are often more black and white and present 'too easy' answers.

Managers modelling and encouraging the right behaviour

Even the most ethical employees need to know that their managers support them to do the right thing.

We have seen the importance of context in determining people's behaviour. We have also seen how people can fail to recognize that a situation may potentially be an ethical issue. If they lack such experience people need to be able to turn to a mentor for help. Managers need to be both role models and mentors. The best test of whether someone does indeed fulfil that role is when people ask 'what would X do?'

It is also important that a person trusts their manager enough to be able to talk to them if they have concerns. So many problems that occur could be nipped in the bud if only they had been discussed early enough for action to be taken. Good managers insist upon this, and have conversations with their people. They signal that they expect that it is better to flag something up that may not turn out to be a problem rather than not address something that could be.

One of the problems that Professor Beer found with the banks that failed in the 2008 financial crisis was that employees did not feel able to speak the truth to those in senior positions. In rare cases, like Paul Moore of HBOS bank, where someone did speak up, they were silenced. So they lacked a 'voice of conscience'. Anyone who was seen trying to get in the way of short-term profits was not popular. In environments like these, those who are inclined to do the wrong thing in pursuit of financial gain are encouraged.

Knowledge

Everyone in the organization needs two particular pieces of knowledge if they are to behave ethically. First, they need to know the rules. If a code of conduct does not exist they need to be told by their manager what the rules are. Second, they need to know who to go to and what to do if they are concerned that a situation might be one of an ethical nature.

Managers and others who are responsible for employees, suppliers and partners also need to know what their personal responsibilities and obligations are in relation to ensuring that others behave ethically. Many of these responsibilities are typically covered in a code of ethics; however, some specific responsibilities including regulatory requirements, investigation procedures and relevant aspects of the law may not be.

Skills

A key skill that managers need to ensure that people are behaving ethically is the ability to have an uncomfortable conversation. By their very nature, ethical dilemmas involve people doing something that they shouldn't be doing. I have found in my work the world over that one of the things that managers find the most difficult and therefore often avoid is raising sensitive issues with people. Conducting a conversation where people may get angry, defensive or upset is something few people relish. To do it well involves a certain amount of courage and a number of skills. The person raising the issue needs to have the interpersonal skills necessary. The first thing they need to do is to plan the conversation in terms of the outcome they want. It is not possible of course to prejudge what the other person will say but it is possible to ask questions in order to achieve a certain objective from the conversation. For example, if the outcome is to understand a sequence of events, the person instigating the conversation needs to keep that in mind in the way they manage the conversation and ask questions. They also need to be able to stay calm and not back away from the conversation if the other person becomes angry or upset. A good deal of skill is also needed in managing your own emotional reaction if you are the instigator of the conversation. I have seen many examples of this being done badly. It goes something like this. The manager raises a 'difficult' issue and the employee becomes upset and defensive. The manager starts to talk too much out of nervousness and tells the employee 'this is really difficult for me too'. He is uncomfortable with silence and so talks even more instead of posing the right questions, giving the employee time to answer and not getting drawn into the emotion of the situation. It does not take long before the manager has lost control of the situation and it becomes a defensive exchange. It is easy to see why most managers prefer to avoid this kind of encounter. But it is crucial that the organization helps them to develop the necessary skills and supports them with a mentor (which could be their own manager, someone from HR or someone else who is skilled at handling such situations). Failure to confront issues because of a fear of the 'difficult conversation' leads to more situations turning into problems than is necessary and the accumulative detrimental effect of lack of competence in this area is underestimated.

A 'learning' mindset

What does a 'learning' mindset mean? It means a predisposition to, and skill in, reflecting and analysing what went well, what didn't and making changes accordingly. It also means a willingness to admit mistakes and see them as an opportunity to do things better. A learning mindset is predicated on an acknowledgement that one isn't and doesn't have to be perfect. Arrogant people and those with overinflated egos block their own learning because they have to be right and they view making a mistake as a sign of weakness.

Few organizations are very competent when it comes to learning. Their cultures reward outcomes not mistakes. This outcome focus is inherent in the education system which rewards results not the process by which the student achieved those results. Carol Dweck[1] describes this phenomenon and its serious negative consequences.

The implications for a non-learning mindset are obvious. People tend to cover up mistakes so they and the organization do not learn from them. They focus on the ends instead of the means. The classic example is the sales person who brings in large revenues but by using sometimes questionable tactics.

The net result is an organization that rewards outcomes irrespective of how those outcomes are achieved. In addition there is little or no knowledge of areas of ethical risk because problems are covered up by employees who are afraid to admit to mistakes.

Finally, and crucially, an organization with a learning mindset understands that ethics cannot be taught, they can only be learned. Think of it this way. If you ask someone to run a training session for colleagues on how to be an ethical manager, this means he has to research the material, think it through and then figure out a way of imparting that knowledge. Who do you think learns more in the class – the trainer or the attendees of the class? The process of learning by discovery, or 'inquiry-based' learning, is far more effective than passively consuming 'content' from a teacher. The teacher's job in an inquiry learning environment is not to provide knowledge or content, but to help the learner to discover knowledge and gain insight for themselves.

This is basic learning theory and has been understood for many years, yet is often not put into practice. When it comes to ethics training the classic example is the introduction of codes of conduct. Many organizations run workshops where someone briefs colleagues on the content of the code and their responsibilities. This is not a very effective way of having employees learn and buy into something. Instead, offering them the right kind of guidance and questions ensures that they grapple with the issues for themselves and so learn, remember far more and, crucially, get to grips with the nature of ethics than any amount of training will deliver.

The very nature of ethical dilemmas means that it is not possible to present managers with a step one, two and three guide. This means that it is arguably the issue that most requires managers to have a strong learning mindset if they are to become competent in it. Designing training course in the way outlined above, that is as a process of inquiry, is a far more effective way of ensuring managers become competent managers of ethics.

A code of conduct

Having a formal code of conduct is important to complement an already ethical culture. Around 40% of respondents in the 'Ethics in the Workplace' Survey said that it is important for an organization to have a code of conduct but less than 30% of the organizations they worked for had one.

Having a code of conduct in place does not guarantee ethical behaviour though. Rules and regulations of any kind are useful to clarify and codify the required behaviours but they will not make ethical people out of unethical ones.

The difference between organizations' espoused ethics and values and their actions can be great. BAE, a British defence and aerospace company, had a global code of conduct in place at the time of the revelations in 2009/10 of bribery and corruption on a massive scale. The code stated that 'leaders will act ethically, promote ethical conduct both within the company and in the markets in which we operate.'

BAE is not the only organization to demonstrate a huge gap between corporate talk and action. KPMG, a large global accountancy and consulting company, also has a code of conduct that makes statements that they have been shown not to live up to 'acting lawfully and ethically, and encouraging this behaviour in the marketplace…maintaining independence and objectivity, and avoiding conflicts of interest'. In 2005 they were found to have created an organizational structure to devise tax avoidance and tax evasion schemes. The firm was fined $456m for 'criminal wrongdoing' and the managers involved were found guilty of tax evasion.

UBS, a global bank, is another company that espoused high ethical standards. They had a code of conduct that stated 'UBS upholds the law, respects regulations and behaves in a principled way. UBS is self-aware and has the courage to face the truth. UBS maintains the highest ethical standards'. In 2009 they were fined $780m by the US authorities for facilitating tax evasion. In early 2010 the company issued a new code of conduct and business ethics which all employees are required to sign. The code addresses issues such as financial crime, competition, confidentiality and human rights issues. The code details the potential sanctions against employees who violate it. The sanctions include warnings, demotions or dismissal. The chairman of the company, Kaspar Villiger, and the CEO, Oswald J. Grüber, have stated that the code is 'an integral part of changing the way UBS conducts business'.

The cases of BAE, KPMG and UBS are examples of companies whose culture and structure permitted, if not promoted, unethical and illegal activities. This is not changed with the introduction of a code of conduct. The best a code of conduct can do is to clarify the obvious dos and don'ts and alert employees to how they should approach different types of scenarios. Some also provide a confidential helpline for people to call for guidance (only around 10% of respondents to the 'Ethics in the Workplace' Survey had access to an ethics helpline at work). A helpline also enables the organization to monitor the kinds of issues that are arising.

However, a code of conduct does not help when an employee does not realize that they could be dealing with a potentially ethical issue in the first place. If they are inexperienced or simply do not have particularly high ethical standards themselves they pose a risk to the organization.

CODE OF CONDUCT

If the organization already has a code of conduct or an ethical policy presumably the standards of behaviour have been defined and articulated. This is usually done by a small group of senior people and rarely involves a wider group of leaders. The challenge comes when communicating the code and getting support for it in the wider organization. There can be an inherent resistance to being told how to behave. Presenting people with 'rules to be followed' can have the effect of creating resistance which then needs to be overcome – and is why this is not a recommended approach.

However, if a code does already exist there are ways of maximizing support for it when 'rolling it out' (see the section on 'process' below).

There are a number of subjects that a code of conduct should cover depending upon the type of organization and the products and services that it provides. Let's take a look at the content of a code of conduct. Below are the sections and topics that it would typically cover:

- An introduction that talks about what a code of conduct is and why it is important to the company.
- Ethical principles (with definitions) that the company wants people to follow such as honesty, openness and accountability.
- Who the code of conduct applies to (usually includes employees, suppliers and partners).
- Who is responsible for what? This section typically talks about management responsibilities and employees' responsibilities.
- Where should a person go for advice and guidance? This section talks about the various options open to an employee and typically includes managers, human resources and the legal department. Some organizations also provide an ethics helpline.

- A decision 'checker'. The most useful codes of conduct include a practical decision-making checklist. The checklist helps employees to decide whether they are handling a situation according to the organization's ethical standards as well as whether they are making the right decision. Such a checklist includes questions like these but, in my experience of codes of conduct, is not usually comprehensive enough (see 'Decision-making framework' in Chapter 1):
  - Is my decision consistent with the organization's ethical principles and code of conduct?
  - Am I setting a good example to others?
  - Would I be confident explaining my decision to my boss, colleagues and family?
  - Would I be happy for my decision to be written about in a newspaper?
  - Have I consulted with others who have expert knowledge to check that my course of action is the best one?
    The idea is that if the employee answers no, or is not sure that they should consult someone else, they minimize the chances of making the wrong decision.
- A business responsibilities section covering issues like bidding for work, contracting with customers and suppliers, share-dealing and inside information, responsibilities towards customers and consumers, consumer safety, trade restrictions, lobbying and political activity and legal and regulatory requirements.

- A guidance section covering situations that employees may come across and how they should respond. This section covers issues like inappropriate behaviour, e.g. bullying, financial matters such as accounting and expenses, use of IT and the Internet, intellectual property, health and safety, environmental issues, the behaviour of suppliers and customers, conflicts of interest, gift giving/acceptance and bribes.
- An index. A code of conduct has to be user-friendly – the whole idea is that employees can turn to it for guidance. Ideally the code will be available online so that searching is easy and employees can access it from their mobile device wherever they are.

The development and introduction of a code of conduct

A process for effectively introducing a code of conduct is as follows.

If you already have a code of conduct the positive thing is that you have already established the standards of behaviour that are expected. The downside, as mentioned above, is that it can be tough to get active support when a code is presented as a *fait accompli*.

The way to gain support is by *not* focusing on the code. This may sound counterintuitive but the best way to gain support from people is to *involve* them not *dictate* to them. This means that you need to be open to changing aspects of the code of conduct depending upon what the employee feedback is. The number of employees you have will determine how big this task is. If your organization is small you will be able to involve everyone, if it is large then you will need a group of representatives that is a manageable size.

Essentially you need to have a structured conversation with everyone about ethics. The inherent complexity of the subject means that it is easy for people to be simplistic when thinking about what should be included in a code. A way to avoid this is to give them some examples of other codes of conduct and facilitate a conversation that helps them to learn about the nature of ethics, their own experiences of ethical dilemmas and ways in which organizations can develop an ethical culture. In other words, help them to think about the context and issues at stake. Only then is it possible to come up with a set of 'rules' that can be contained in a code of conduct.

Once such conversations are completed the content can be fed into the existing code of conduct and adapted to reflect the views of employees. In practice, it is unlikely that the standards that senior management think appropriate are all that different from those that employees think appropriate. The key is having a good structure and facilitation for the conversations and not to start with a blank sheet but to give people topics to discuss with key questions to address.

Done well this process can mean not just buy-in but a real pride that the organization is one with high ethical standards and aspirations.

I saw this for myself in a pharmaceutical company where it came over loud and clear that everyone believed the organization was ethical and took pride in that fact. The code of conduct *per se* was less important as a set of standards of behaviour, it was more important as a symbol of the organization's commitment to being ethical. Having a process to engage and involve employees is the key to commitment to ethics and pride in working for an organization that takes ethics so seriously. Otherwise at best it is a document that people refer to when they have a problem and if they remember about it. At worst it is something that is never referred to other than by those who created it.

THE CHALLENGES OF CREATING AN ETHICAL CULTURE

Some of the characteristics that lead to an ethical culture are easier to embed than others. And some of the characteristics are dependent upon others of the characteristics being present. The successful application of each of the characteristics depends upon others working effectively. An ethical culture is the result of all the elements in the following table being in place and working well.

The Ethical Ecosystem

	Ethical culture
	↑
Behaviours	Learning from mistakes.
	Speaking up when something is believed to be wrong.
	Challenging unethical behaviour.
	↑
Skills	Mentoring.
	Handling ethical dilemmas including conducting difficult conversations.
	↑
Knowledge	The rules (code of conduct).
	The importance of ethics and implications of ethical transgressions (organizationally and personally).
	How to manage an ethical dilemma.
	That the organization will support those who speak up against unethical practice.
	↑
Attitudes	Responsibility.
	'Learning' mindset.
	Courage to confront wrongdoing.
	Internal locus of control.
	↑
Values	Managers as role models.
	Hiring the right people.
	Doing the right thing.
	↑
Purpose and meaning	Ethical leadership.
	Vision.

Each of the characteristics on the right side of this table is part of the 'Ethical Ecosystem'. Each part of the system needs to be working well in order to create the required outcome, i.e. an ethical culture. The job of the leaders in an organization is to constantly pay attention to each of these elements of the system in order to correct and adjust pieces that are not working in service of the greater purpose. A good analogy is the job of an airline pilot. There are numerous factors that need to be working well. His job is to keep an eye on the big picture, in his case flying the plane safely from a to b, as well as all the individual parts of the system and their interaction.

Thinking in this systemic way about organizational ethics makes it easier to understand how an ethical culture is created. It becomes clear that introducing a code of ethics will only be effective if the elements below it in the table are in place. Otherwise it is like building a house on shaky foundations.

It is very attractive and compelling to bosses to focus on creating initiatives at the 'knowledge' level because it is relatively easy and tangible. It is easy to tick that box. And of course it fits with the need for regulation and that is important. So all in all it feels good and instils a sense of relief that the ethical thing is being taken care of. But it can create a false sense of security.

Bosses often also think of ethics as a question of a one-off implementation. It is actually an ongoing social practice. A 'social practice' because it spans the boundaries of home and work – at its core it is about personal values and moral code. It is about constant learning, questioning and grappling. It is essentially about an ongoing inner dialogue on the subject of how, as a leader, you want to live your life and run your organization.

Consider the examples of unethical practice and corporate scandals in this book. If running an ethical organization really mattered to the bosses in these examples they would be the sort of people who actively engaged with their own ethics. They would also most probably struggle to a certain degree. Essentially they would be approaching engaging with ethics as a verb. That is they would see that ethics is a result of ongoing action. It is a process. And, by definition, a process is ongoing. If they did all that they would have paid attention to the inadequacies of their organizations that resulted in these scandals. Put simply, if the boss doesn't care about ethics the danger is that no one else will and at best the organization will pay lip service to it. The use of a practical and systematic approach to building an ethical culture not only increases your chances of success but also demonstrates that you are serious about it.

Each element shown in the Ethical Ecosystem doesn't just happen. It comes into being if supported on an ongoing basis with a variety of tools as well as the commitment of the senior leadership. The third column in the table below shows the tools that are necessary to support the corresponding elements of ethical culture development.

The Ethical Ecosystem

Ethical culture

↑

Behaviours	Learning from mistakes.
	Speaking up when something is believed to be wrong.
	Challenging unethical behaviour.

↑

Skills	Mentoring.
	Handling ethical dilemmas including conducting difficult conversations.

↑

Knowledge	The rules (code of conduct).
	The importance of ethics and implications of ethical transgressions (organizationally and personally).
	How to manage an ethical dilemma.
	That the organization will support those who speak up against unethical practice.

↑

Attitudes	Responsibility.
	'Learning' mindset.
	Courage to confront wrongdoing.
	Internal locus of control.

↑

Values	Managers as role models.
	Hiring the right people.
	Doing the right thing.

↑

Purpose and meaning	Ethical leadership.
	Vision.

Essential tools

Mentoring.

Decision-making framework.

Code of conduct and development/introduction process.

Employees' workshop.

Ethical leadership development programme.

CHAPTER 6

The Future of Ethics

What this chapter will do for you:

- Increase your awareness of some of the issues that will have an impact on the future of ethics in organizations
- Stimulate your thinking about what changes you might want to make in your own professional practice and/or your organization

The David Hare play *The Power of Yes* explores how the global financial system came to collapse in 2008. The play builds a damning case against the bankers who were blinded by greed and the love of the deal ('the thing itself'). Myron Scholes, inventor of a 'foolproof' mathematical investment equation, is a key character in the play. In 1997 he won the Nobel Prize; in 1998 his hedge fund went bust and he was later arrested for tax evasion. Fred Goodwin, the former head of Royal Bank of Scotland, features heavily too with his unrepentant greed and compulsive deal-making. As a key protagonist in the banking crisis and having cost the tax payer billions he walked away having personally earned £30 m in his ten years with RBS and with a huge annual pension.

David Hare's story of those involved in the financial crisis paints a picture of self-serving individuals who followed the age-old path of hubris followed by nemesis. Sadly the script does not seem far fetched, nor does Hare exaggerate or drama-tize events and the actions of individuals. The play is more like an explanation of events by interviewing or analysing the actions of key players.

There is no reason to expect that blatantly self-serving indi-viduals like those who featured in the play will be motivated to change and create ethical enterprises. Those that have refused to take any responsibility for their part in the collapse of the banking system in 2008 are unlikely to change. Of course it is to be hoped that business leaders like these are in the minority. It does make you wonder though how many of those who have the drive and ambition to get to the top of corporations are motivated by their own ambition as opposed to wanting to leave a legacy that benefits a wider group. The qualities needed to get to the top of organizations need to be re-thought. The ambition and drive needed to reach very senior positions, while a strength on the way up, can become a weakness. When ambition turns into self-serving motivations and success creates overinflated egos the risks to the organization are great. The typical profile of a CEO needs to be re-examined in the light of some of the characteristics of those who presided over the downfall of the banks and other organizations that have been found guilty of illegal, unethical or negligent practice.

KEY CONSIDERATIONS FOR THE COMING DECADES

The future of ethics in business depends upon a number of key factors. These factors serve as an indication to organizations of what they need to focus on if they are to be successful for the long term.

- A new kind of CEO who can run an organization ethically because it's the right thing to do, not in order just to adhere to regulations or enhance their reputation.
- Balancing stakeholder needs, not just focusing on creating shareholder value.
- Consumers and customers and the extent to which they demand higher standards of ethics by choosing to do business only with those that they believe to be ethical.
- The younger generation of leaders and how they choose to run their organizations in the future.
- The influence of the media and the Internet.
- Business schools and their willingness to embrace ethical education as a fundamental requirement of management.

A new kind of CEO

More than 80% of respondents to the 'Ethics in the Workplace' Survey 2010 answered 'because it is morally right' to the question 'In your view why is it important for organizations to be ethical?'

Ethical organizations are usually that way because those that run them have high moral values. I interviewed a number of CEOs for this book and they all run their companies in an ethical way purely because they believe it was right, irrespective of how much it cost the company or whether there was any personal risk in doing so. Without exception, they pointed only to their values and morals when explaining to me why ethics was important. It will be these kinds of leaders – the ones who see regulatory requirements only as a minimum level of aspiration – that will set the standard for ethical organizations of the future.

In the wake of the damage to the reputation of business following numerous corporate scandals and the 2008 financial crisis some ethically minded CEOs may feel a new determination to restore the public's faith in business. The worst of the self-serving contemporary business leaders like Fred Goodwin have highlighted the damaging effects of self-serving leadership on organizations.

We are now entering a new age where trust and reputation are more important than ever before. The public have had enough of hearing about errant business leaders.

Consumers and employees will vote with their feet and organizations that don't have great reputations will lose out on top talent as well as customers. It won't be good enough for leaders to view trust as a means to an end. People are far more discerning now than ever before – they can distinguish the genuine from the corporate spin. Gone are the days when empty advertising campaigns and surface-level employer branding worked. The organizations that lack real trust and purely use PR as a means of gaining it will not succeed any more. It's not that consumers and employees expect organizations to be perfect but they do expect them to be honest. Values-based leadership, while it may be at a premium now, will be incredibly sought after. Even organizations that are more concerned with risk management than doing the right thing for the sake of it will want to hire those with a good ethical track record. Reputation is everything these days and individual and organizational reputation is valuable currency.

Balancing stakeholder needs

In the past, the unquestioned mantra of business has been to create value for its shareholders. From the perspective of employees and customers, it is rather a narrow and somewhat uninspiring goal. Nevertheless it is what business schools teach and what most business leaders live by. Philosophical questions such as 'what is business for?' have had no place in the boardroom. Perhaps that will continue to be the case but in this post-financial crisis era there is far more call from a whole range of stakeholders for businesses to do good and do the right thing as well as to make money.

Today stakeholders' demands are more strident. Business leaders are going to have to work harder to sustain their confidence and trust. If organizations don't maintain trust their very survival will be at risk. Stakeholders are increasingly demanding that business broadens its remit beyond the pure profit motive. Simply creating shareholder value is not enough. They are going to need to actively contribute to society by doing good.

Doing good and doing the right thing clearly mean different things in different industries. In pharmaceuticals a new era has dawned and at the time of writing the whole industry is in the midst of massive change. Just about every pharmaceutical company talks about putting the patients first. In banking it is about encouraging responsible spending and investment and in retail it is serving the customer while minimizing damage to the planet. All industry sectors have their own version of these 'beyond profit' goals. A cynic might say that this is nothing new and the so-called 'corporate social responsibility' movement is all about incorporating public interest into the business agenda. The problem is that many organizations have adopted corporate social responsibility (CSR) principles in a tokenistic, 'tick-box' way. They have used it as a shallow attempt to bolster reputation.

The basic premise of CSR is that long-term benefit to society should not be compromised in favour of short-term gain. CSR is voluntary and is undertaken by some organizations and not others. Some embrace it because they genuinely believe it to be right; others do it to gain PR advantage.

Business will increasingly be called upon to go beyond adherence to laws and regulations. They will need to take responsibility for the impact of their activities on the environment, consumers, employees, communities and all other affected groups. They will also be expected to actively participate in contributing to the well-being of the communities that they have direct and indirect impact upon. In this way ethical business takes on a much broader meaning – it encompasses not just how a business is run but how it hurts or helps society.

The call for organizations to become more socially responsible can only increase as consumer awareness and concern increases and the brightest and best workers opt to work for the organizations with the best reputations. The connection between ethical business and corporate social responsibility can only become stronger. To genuinely care about being socially responsible means embracing a desire to do good beyond the walls of the enterprise. This underpinning *raison d'être* is true of some organizations in the private sector and not true of others. Indeed some companies actively cause damage in the course of their mission and in the process of making money.

All of this highlights the importance of a desire and capability to make the right decisions for the long-term sustainability of the organization and not just for short-term gain. To rebuild lost trust CEOs will have to demonstrate their commitment to their organization's survival beyond their tenure. They will be called to account for much more than profit and they will need to be clear about their strategy, understand the workings of their organizations, and treat financial performance as a lagging indicator of success not as a primary driver of strategy.

The demands of consumers and customers

The idea of ethical purchasing is now well established in the Western world.

The UK's Co-operative Bank's Ethical Consumerism Report 2009 noted that the UK ethical goods market was worth £36bn in 2008 compared to £13.5bn in 1999. The market for ethical banking and investments tripled in size and was worth £14.35bn in 2008.

Concerned consumers are increasingly favouring ethical organizations and make buying decisions based on ethical considerations. There is also much more of an awareness of unethical marketing practices such as falsification of data, targeting vulnerable groups with harmful products (e.g. tobacco) and misleading advertising.

Scandals like the deliberate contamination of baby milk by its manufacturers have understandably caused outrage and cynicism among consumers about companies and governments. After initial denial by the Chinese government, it conducted an investigation and found that 21 companies were guilty of this practice. The companies had been adding melamine to milk and infant formula to make it appear to have a higher protein content. Six children died and more than 800 were hospitalized as a result of consuming the milk products. The World Health Organization said that it was the biggest incident of its kind that it had to deal with in years.

In a speech in March 2001, Dr Gro Harlem Brundtland, Director-General of the World Health Organization, listed some of the serious incidents in the previous years including dioxins in poultry in Belgium in 1999, an incident of toxic mustard seed oil in India in 1998 which led to a number of reported deaths and the case of toxic cooking oil in Spain in 1981 resulting in 800 deaths.

He commented that incidents like these appear in the media, but that the more serious health hazards posed by chemicals in food are chronic and often build up over time; it is impossible for the consumer to avoid them and they are often without immediate symptoms. His view is that the only way to protect consumers from chemical hazards is by proper government intervention. In matters of public safety regulation and government intervention are critical. But so are the motives of food manufacturers. As long as profit for shareholders trumps public safety, there will be risk. The process by which food gets onto supermarket shelves is complex and there are many organizations in the supply chain. It is impossible to police the whole supply chain. But commitment to and observance of ethical practice is the most powerful guardian of public good. This goes for all types of organization not just food companies.

The trend for consumers to hold big business accountable is likely to continue and possibly increase in its intensity. Ethics and ethical practices are going to become more important and will increasingly become the drivers of success. The organizations that survive and thrive are going to be those that take the views and values of its customers seriously and who are committed to the greater long-term good of all stakeholders.

The young generation of leaders

There are some that say the young generation is more likely to compromise ethical standards than their older counterparts are. They cite an increase in downloading illegally from the Internet, exam plagiarism and misrepresentation on job applications.

Others point to the fact that the younger generation (so-called Generation Y, born between 1980 and 1994, and Generation Z, born between 1995 and 2009) is more informed about social, environmental and political ethics. The school curriculum in some countries now contains ethics-related issues such as citizenship, which therefore, in theory, allows the younger generation to grow up to be more socially conscious.

It is of course impossible to generalize and dangerous to stereotype. It may be that older generations have more of a moral conscience because they were influenced by stricter upbringings or religion. Religion was certainly a major influence on moral code and standards. They grew up in a world where 'being good and obedient' was emphasized more than being questioning and challenging authority was. The education system and parenting styles in many countries today encourage children to challenge and to think for themselves. And of course there is less religious influence generally.

Young people entering the workplace expect and value openness and trust. Their older colleagues were conditioned not to expect their bosses to be open and share information. In the days before email, instant messaging and SMS, communication was very limited in comparison to today. The common mantra for whether or not to share information and knowledge was 'on a need to know basis' – in other words, tell as few people as possible. This has changed as transparency has increased.

Organizations like Wikipedia and eBay have proved a new way of working based on trust and self-regulation. Business models like these have challenged the 'central control' mentality that has existed since industrialization first brought people into factories. The older generations still relate to organizations as hierarchical structures. The ways of working, getting on, sharing information and making decisions are all dictated by, and invariably constrained by, the hierarchy. The traditional Western family units were hierarchical with father at the top, followed by mother and children at the bottom. This has changed too. Nowadays the family unit is more of a democracy with children being consulted about and involved in family decisions and not subjected to the dominant rule of the father. It's no surprise that young people today, having experienced democratic-style involvement in the family and in education, have a shock when they encounter the less democratic world of organizations. They certainly don't understand or accept hierarchical structures in the way that their older colleagues have been conditioned to do.

The younger generation is less likely to be nervous of speaking up against wrongdoing. A workforce that feels able to freely confront and challenge, without fear of retribution, is a key component of an ethical culture, and as business leaders of the future will decide how businesses are run in the coming years.

The media and the Internet

Over the past few decades people's privacy has gradually been eroded by the media. In the past the mainstream media's decision to publish rested on the editorial test of whether an individual's failings affected their public responsibilities. John F. Kennedy was an example of this. In his day the media were less concerned with public figures' personal lives. Had he been in public office today the media would have had a feeding frenzy over his infidelities.

The 'rules' about the relevance of private details upon public duties have all but evaporated. Extra-marital affairs, drug use and sexuality all seem to be deemed as relevant, presumably because they indicate something of a person's character. There is nothing that is off-limits to today's media and this means that any breach of ethics is exposed and thus reputation is risked. This may well mean that the selection criteria of senior people in organizations will take account of their ethical record and values. Board members will be keen to protect their own reputation so are very likely to start taking ethical considerations much more seriously.

The other main way in which the media has changed is that we no longer rely on journalists or news organizations for news. So-called 'citizen journalism' means that anyone can report news – all it takes is access to the Internet. The first pictures of the tsunami disaster in 2004 in South-East Asia and the London bombings in July 2005 came from citizens who were using their mobile devices to take photographs and video footage. Because these people were on the scene their reportage was obviously better than any news agency could offer. Non-professional 'reporters' include bloggers and other social media reporters. Their news can travel very fast via the Internet and, for better or worse, there are no editors filtering the content.

There are of course ethical issues that apply to these amateur reporters as there have always been to those who have done it as a living and have, to a greater or lesser degree, embraced a sense of professional accountability. Now the ethical decisions rest with each person and are impossible to regulate. This will inevitably mean problems as some will be guilty of unethical reporting. But it will also have the effect of raising a general awareness in society of our own individual ethical responsibilities.

Business schools

The first MBA (Masters Degree in Business Administration) was run at Harvard Business School in 1908. The aim was to formally train professional managers to run large organizations. Social responsibility was strongly advocated as there was a belief then that big business should be managed for the long-term public good and not for short-term gains.

After World War Two thinking began to change. Nobel Prize winning economist Milton Friedman's theories started to change business thinking toward a view that markets are self-regulating and the business leader's job was to maximize shareholder value.

Critics of this philosophy of business argue that it has been a contributor if not cause of so many problems including the 2008 banking crisis. In his 2007 book on the history of MBAs, Harvard Business School professor R. Khurana[1] concludes that business schools have veered from their original purpose of 'training managers to rule in the name of society'. University-based business schools were founded to train a professional class of managers in the mould of doctors and lawyers but have effectively retreated from that goal, leaving a gaping moral hole at the centre of business education and perhaps in management itself.

The focus of many MBA programmes has tended to be on quantitative methods and mathematical models, including the use of advanced analysis. It is a fairly reductionist, 'spreadsheet' view of running a business. This is fine if it is balanced with a recognition of the importance of long-term effects of decisions and the moral duty of business not just the profit motive.

MBA-style thinking has given students the illusion of being able to control all financial risk. Critics of the MBA approach point to this weakness as well as a failure to equip students to make good all-round judgements encompassing considerations of social responsibility as well as profit and growth. Ethics and ethical decision making has not historically been a feature of the MBA course and when it is it is usually an additional study instead of a core part of the curriculum.

Change is afoot though and business schools are increasingly recognizing the need for values-based management practice. Oaths akin to the doctors' Hippocratic Oath are being adopted by some students and business schools particularly in the USA. This is the Thunderbird School of Global Management Oath of Honor:

I will strive to act with honesty and integrity. I will respect the rights and dignity of all people. I will strive to create sustainable prosperity worldwide. I will oppose all forms of corruption and exploitation. And I will take responsibility for my actions. As I hold true to these principles, it is my hope that I may enjoy an honorable reputation and peace of conscience.

It is questionable whether having students take an oath like this will make any difference to whether they behave ethically. But it gets the issue onto the agenda and may even mean that MBA courses appeal to a broader group of people than they have until now. It is a sign that those offering executive education will increasingly be expected to take the subject seriously and not treat it as an add-on.

The opportunity for business schools today is to prepare executives to shape and change business towards a more sustainable model. To do that it has to embrace ethics, values, critical thinking beyond the numbers and long-term strategic perspective over short-term gains.

Howard Gardner[2] of the Harvard Graduate School of Education wrote of the ethical mind:

> An ethical mind broadens respect for others into something more abstract. A person with an ethical mind asks herself, "What kind of a person, worker and citizen do I want to be? If all workers in my profession adopted the mindset I have, or if everyone did what I do, what would the world be like?

In summary, there could well be a 'perfect storm' of individuals, businesses and educators realizing that on an individual as well as an organizational level ethics does matter and needs to be at the centre of organizations' agendas. This realization may come from a desire to move away from 'bad' things such as corporate scandals, effects on people and the planet of misusing resources or just a perception of a general decline in moral standards. It may also be a desire to move towards better things – positive contribution to society and local communities, harmonious relationships at work and the pride and peace of mind that comes from a good reputation.

Whatever the case, it appears that the forces are strong and the future of ethics is clear. There will be less tolerance – from regulators and law makers as well as citizens – of those that behave unethically. Ethical organizations will continue to attract the best people. In contrast, those that are perceived as lacking in ethical standards will be left behind in a world that is demanding greater social responsibility from big business.

There has never before been a time where the individual has the potential to have such a big influence on business. In a global economy where business leaders are concerned about being able to attract the best talent, the balance of power has shifted to the employee. Great people are in demand and will choose to work for excellent organizations with the best reputations. Consumers are more informed than ever before due to the Internet. They now have access to a huge amount of information and insight about organizations including comparison websites. Tales of negative consumer experiences travel fast as do companies' responses to customer complaints. The consumer has more power than ever before and can exert pressure on organizations to change.

Reputation has always been a valuable asset for an individual and for an organization. It is fast becoming a major source of competitive advantage. Before too long, proof of competence in handling ethical issues and attendance on an ethical leadership programme will be sought-after aspects of a person's résumé.

Maybe your organization is already a leading light in the world of business ethics. Perhaps it supports you in the development of your ethical knowledge and skills. If this is not the case, there are huge advantages for you in taking responsibility for increasing your own capability in this arena. Doing the right thing could save your reputation as well as enhancing it.

Appendix: Summary of Ethics in the Workplace Survey 2010

As part of the research for this book I conducted a global survey of 315 respondents – the 'Ethics in the Workplace' Survey 2010. The aim of the survey was to gain insight into the attitudes, opinions and experiences of people of ethics in the workplace.

This appendix contains details of the survey respondents and a summary of some of the key findings.

THE RESPONDENTS

Total number of respondents: 315 (49% male, 51% female)

Ages

9% aged between 18 and 30

35% aged between 31 and 45

52% aged between 46 and 64

4% aged over 65

Country

62% from UK

7% from Europe

24% from North America

7% from the rest of the world (includes Caribbean, India, China, Australia, New Zealand, Asia other and Middle East)

Sector

69% work in the private sector

27% work in the public sector

6% work in the not for profit

(a few respondents work in both, hence the total is more than 100%)

Size of organization

Respondents work in organizations of the following sizes:

35% fewer than 50 employees

7% 51 to 150 employees

14% 151 to 1,000 employees

11% 1,001 to 3,000 employees

12% 3,001 to 10,000 employees

21% more than 10,000 employees

Industry sectors

Academic 10%

Banking, finance and insurance 9%

Education 5%

Law/legal services 3%

Media/printing/publishing 8%

Pharmaceutical 3%

Business, professional services, consulting 20%

Public sector (including NHS, police, emergency services and social services) 12%

Not for profit 6%

Technology and Internet 6%

Other (includes airline, automotive, communications/PR, construction, hotel and leisure, research, retail, telecommunications and transportation/logistics) 18%

Managers/non-managers

51% manage others

19% manage people sometimes

30% don't manage others

HEADLINE FINDINGS

The survey results indicate that handling ethical issues is a very real and frequently extremely challenging part of people's work in today's organizations.

Respondents reported a staggering range of ethical situations that they had been faced with. These ranged from very serious and difficult issues involving ethical transgressions by senior managements and bribery cases to plagiarism, sexual harassment, bullying, discrimination, stealing, abusive behaviour and senior managers' unwillingness to tackle ethical issues.

Organizations do not appear to be doing a great job at supporting people to be able to handle these situations. It is hard to say whether that is because they don't realize there could be a problem, whether they do not take it seriously enough, or whether they don't really know how to support people and engender an ethical culture. The survey results suggest that the measures that they are taking are inadequate.

It is worth noting the large number of comments that respondents made, many going into quite a lot of detail about the situations they and others around them had faced. The nature of the comments suggested that people felt strongly about the subject and had challenging experiences themselves, some of an extremely serious nature that put individuals or the organization at significant amount of risk.

SUMMARY OF KEY DATA FROM SURVEY

Have ethical standards in organizations increased, decreased or stayed the same in the last five years?

Responses by age group

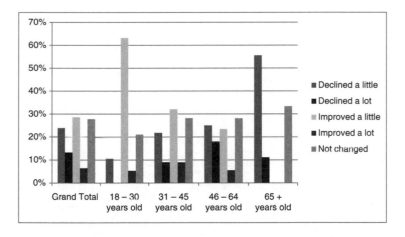

None of the respondents thought that ethical standards have improved a lot over the last five years. This is probably understandable given the number of business and political scandals that the media have reported in recent years. Overall though, respondents in all age groups thought that ethical standards have improved a little with Generation Y (the 18 to 30s) having the highest percentage of respondents believing that to be the case. This is in notable contrast to the over 65s. No respondents from this age group believed that ethical standards had improved at all. Most believed that they have declined a little or not changed. This could be explained by the moral values of that age group. A number of people I interviewed who were over 65 believed that moral standards in organizations have slipped considerably.

Responses by public, private and not-for-profit sectors

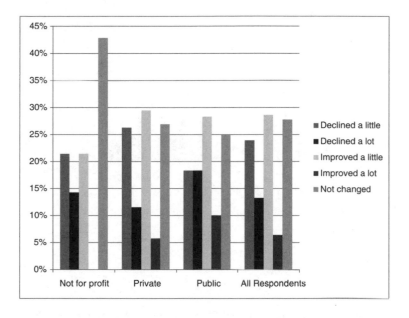

Only a relatively small proportion of respondents in these three sectors believe that ethical standards have declined a lot. However, at least 25% in each group believe that standards have declined a little, but a greater proportion believes that standards have improved. This could be explained by the fact that there has been a lot of reportage on public and private sector scandals and people perhaps assume that regulation and accountability are increasing.

Responses by industry sector

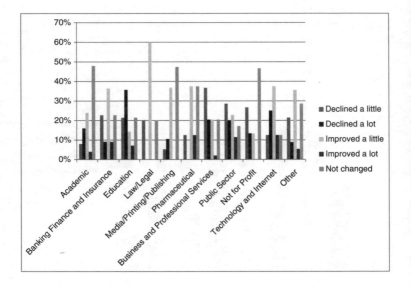

It is interesting, given the 2008 banking crisis, that more than 30% of respondents from banking, finance and insurance and law/legal believe that ethical standards have improved a little and very few believe that they have declined a lot. This could be perhaps be explained by the increase in regulation – respondents could perceive that this has resulted in an increase in ethical standards.

Response by organization size

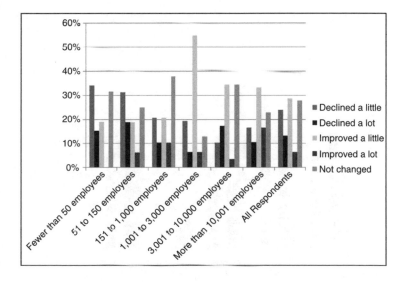

There is not a great deal of difference though in views across all sizes of organization. The only notable point is that the smaller the organization the fewer the proportion of respondents think that ethical standards have improved.

Responses by country

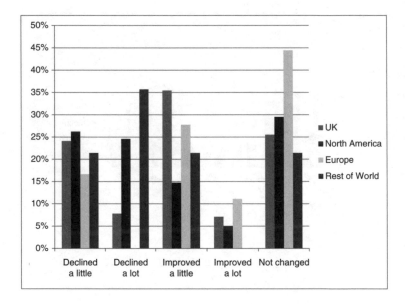

Few respondents in any country believed that ethical standards have improved a lot. 50% of respondents from North America believed that standards have declined a little or a lot whereas in the UK only about 30% of respondents believed that to be the case. This is perhaps surprising given the 2008 banking crisis. A possible explanation why a greater proportion of people do not believe standards have declined is because they think that standards were always quite low but now they have been exposed.

How important is it for organizations to be ethical?

Responses by age

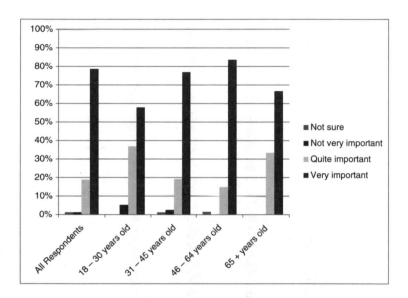

You can see from this chart that the majority of people in all age groups believe that it is important for organizations to be ethical. None of the respondents in the over 45 age bracket believes that it is not important and only a very few in the 18–30 age bracket say that it is not very important.

Responses by public, private and not-for-profit sectors

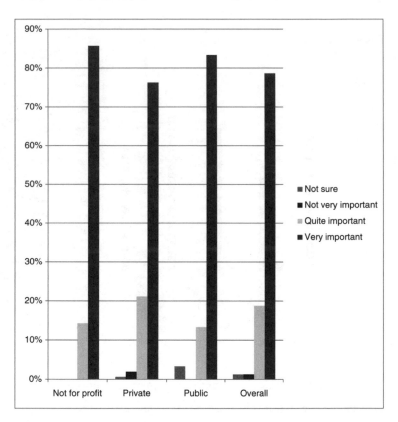

The message is clear here. More than 70% of all respondents believe that it is very important for organizations to be ethical. Probably predictably, a greater proportion of respondents in the public and not-for-profit sectors believe it to be more important than those in the private sector.

Hardly any respondents believe that it is not very important.

Responses by industry sector

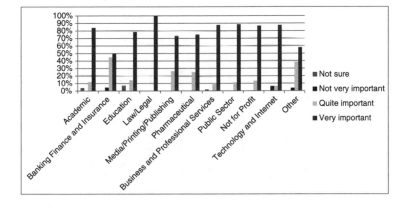

Again, this chart shows that the majority of respondents in all industry sectors believe that it is important for organizations to be ethical. Only a few respondents (in banking, finance and insurance and in technology and Internet) said that it was not important.

Responses by size of organization

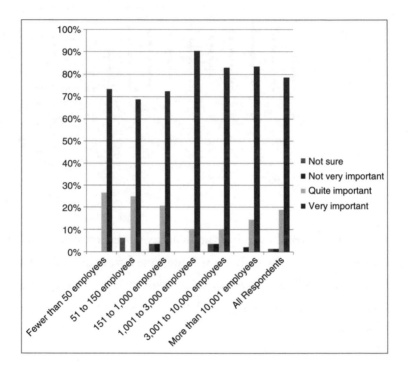

There is little difference in the beliefs of people irrespective of the size of organization they work in – the great proportion believe that it is important for an organization to be ethical.

Responses by country

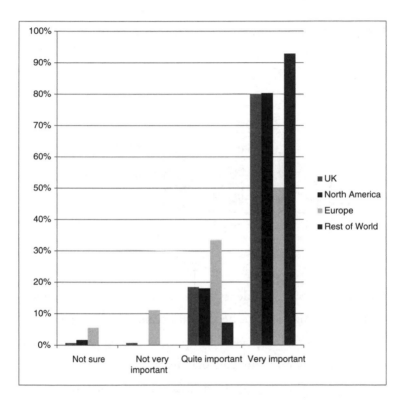

More than 80% of respondents in all countries believed that it is quite or very important for organizations to be ethical.

Why is it important for organizations to be ethical?

Responses by public, private and not-for-profit sectors

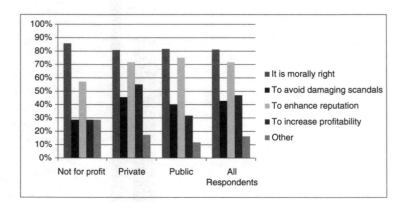

80% or more of respondents in all sectors said that it is important for organizations to be ethical because it is morally right.
Increasing profitability was an important reason for more than
40% of respondents but you may have predicted that to have
been higher. The message from this chart is that most people
believe organizations should be ethical because it is the right
thing rather than for commercial gain.

Responses by age

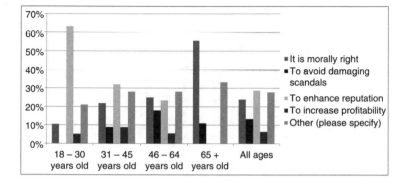

The over 65 age group stand out as believing that it is important for organizations to be ethical because it is morally right. The younger the age group the fewer people believe this to be the case. This would support the belief by some that moral standards are slipping among the young. Interestingly the 18–30s believe that enhancing reputation is a more important factor than any other age groups do.

Responses by industry sector

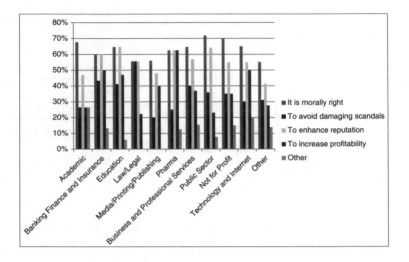

Respondents in different industry sectors believe that organizations should be ethical 'because it is morally right' in all cases with the public sector and not-for-profit being the highest. Increasing profitability was seen as important by a greater proportion of respondents in banking, finance and insurance (50%), technology and Internet (50%) and pharmaceutical (61%). There were three sectors where 60% or more of respondents selected 'to enhance reputation' – education, pharmaceutical and the public sector.

Responses by size of organization

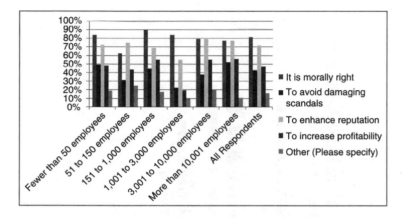

Increasing profitability was cited as important by more than 40% of respondents in all sizes of organization except those that have between 1,001 and 3,000 employees where fewer than 20% said it was important.

Responses by country

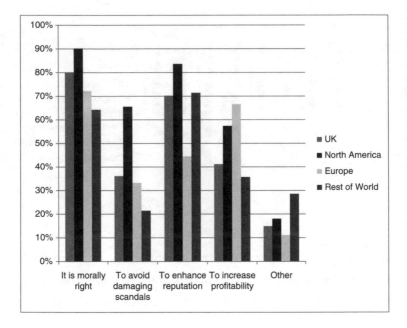

90% of respondents from the USA said that it is important for an organization to be ethical because it is morally right, whereas fewer than 60% chose 'to increase profitability'. Avoiding damaging scandals was chosen as important by a greater proportion of people in the USA (more than 60%) than in the UK (just over 30%) which is a little surprising as both countries have suffered a lot from damaging scandals in the private and public sectors. Americans may be particularly conscious of this though because of the potentially massive costs associated with litigation in the USA.

In the last year how often have you had to deal with a situation of an ethical nature?

Responses by public, private and not-for-profit sectors

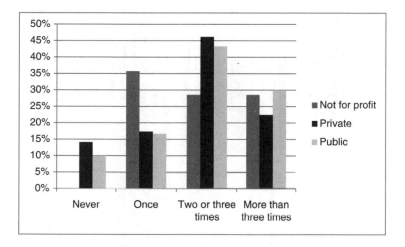

Most respondents have had to deal with a situation of an ethical nature, with those in the private sector having dealt with them more frequently overall.

What was the nature of the ethical dilemmas that you had to deal with?

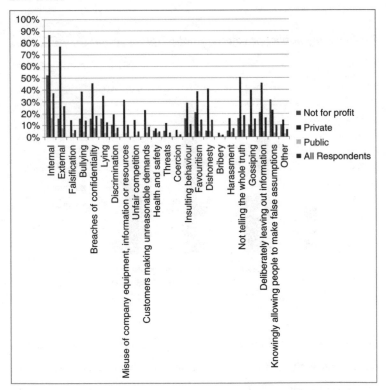

Respondents have dealt with a range of ethical situations, the most common being breaches of confidentiality, bullying, dishonesty, favouritism, gossiping, not telling the whole truth and deliberately leaving out information. It is also interesting to note that it is the more 'subtle' issues (e.g. not telling the whole truth and leaving out information) that people have to deal with than the most obvious issues like falsification. It is clear from the chart that more respondents in the private sector have dealt with most of these issues than their counterparts in the public and not-for-profit sectors have. That doesn't necessarily mean that there are more occurrences of such 'offences' in the private sector; it could be that they are more willing to deal with them or that the expectation of their organizations is such that they have to deal with them.

*When you have dealt with an ethical issue what were the challenges
you encountered?*

Responses by public, private and not-for-profit sectors

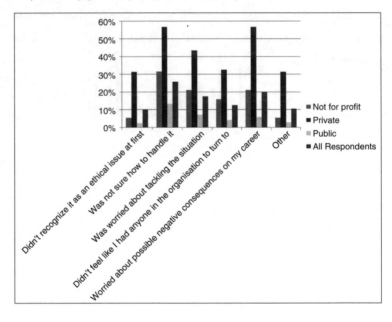

It is striking that more than half of the respondents in the
private sector were not sure how to handle the ethical situations
they had to deal with and that they were worried about the
negative consequences on them or their career. It is perhaps
surprising that so few people in the pubic and not-for-profit
sectors had relatively few challenges. Perhaps that is to do with
clearer procedures in those sectors or a stronger ethic of professional accountability.

What help, if any, did you draw on to help you deal with the ethical situations that you have encountered?

Responses by public, private and not-for-profit sectors

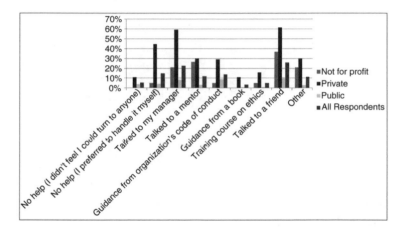

The most common source of help was talking to a friend, particularly among those in the private sector. This could indicate a failure of organizations to have adequate support mechanisms in place. It could also be indicative of the fact that ethical issues are often so sensitive and tricky that people feel more comfortable speaking to friends about them rather than work colleagues. It is striking how few people in the not-for-profit and public sectors turned to their managers for help. And it is perhaps worrying that more than 40% of respondents in the private sector sought no help at all. Guidance in the form of training was rare among respondents in any sector. All of this raises the question as to how much help organizations are really giving their managers in an area of their work that you could argue is the most challenging and presents the most risk to the individual and the organization.

Does your organization's performance review include behaving ethically?

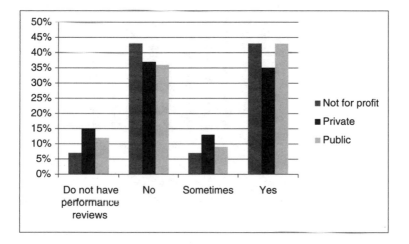

Given the apparent lack of guidance and support that respondents of all sectors experience it is surprising that so many of their organizations include behaving ethically in their performance appraisal. Its presence in a performance appraisal suggests that it is deemed to be important, yet few organizations offer training courses, although more have codes of conduct. Perhaps some organizations believe that a code of conduct is enough.

Which of these do you think are important for an organization to have?

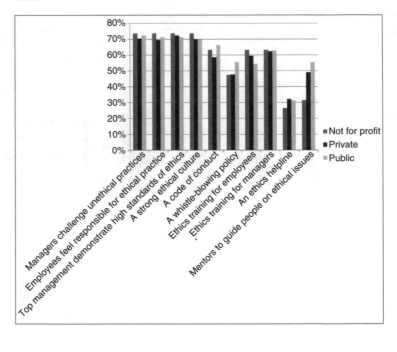

Around 70% or more of respondents in all sectors say it is important for managers to challenge unethical practice, for employees to feel responsible, for top management to demonstrate high standards of ethics and for there to be a strong ethical culture. However, only between 30% and just over 50% of them experience these things in their own organizations. There is a noticeable similarity across sectors in how important people think these different elements are. However, there is more difference when it comes to the different sectors having the various mechanisms in place.

Which of these mechanisms that support an ethical culture does your organization have?

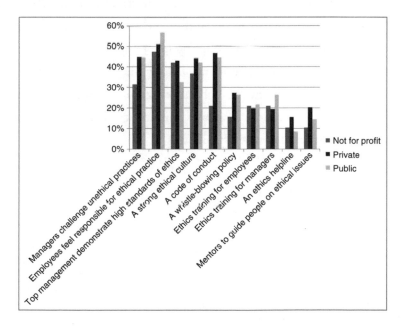

Which organizations and/or sectors do you think have high ethical standards?

The most frequently mentioned organizations were the Bodyshop, John Lewis, Google, Co-op and Johnson and Johnson. The most frequently mentioned sectors were education, not for profit and health/medicine.

A number of respondents said that they felt that very few organizations had very high ethical standards.

Which organizations and/or sectors do you think have low ethical standards?

It is probably not surprising in the aftermath of the 2008 banking collapse that banking and financial services were cited more often than any other as having low ethical standards. The following sectors were also mentioned by many respondents as having low ethical standards: pharmaceutical, estate agents/real estate agents, insurance companies, public service organizations and small or family owned businesses.

OTHER COMMENTS

Finally, people were asked to make any other comments they had relating to ethics at work. An unusually high number of comments were given. There was a high level of engagement from about a third of the survey respondents who were keen to have a dialogue about ethical issues. There is clearly a lot of interest in the issue. People feel strongly about the issues and many reported that they are struggling considerably.

Here are some quotes from the comments people made. They are grouped into key themes:

Leadership

'Need to make sure top management realize their role in practising what they preach and that all company employees understand there are consequences to ethical violations'

'Whether an organization is ethical is totally influenced by the strong ethics of individual leaders'

'Really important, one of my top 4 or 5 factors I would look for in a leader'

'The ethics of an organization will never be any better than those of its leadership – CEOs down to supervisors'

'Ethics comes from the top. When management act ethically it sets the tone for employees and customers'

'There are good and bad in all sectors and it is easy to generalize, but it is the individuals that lead organizations who have the greatest impact on their employees by the example they set and standards they expect of their employees'

Training

'In my experience people don't think about these issues unless stimulated to do so, so discussion is a good thing to engage in'

'It will become more important to educate or train in what is OK and not OK, i.e. ethics as guidance via family background will have increasingly less effect on an increasing majority of young professionals coming through into commerce'

Culture

'It is very important and needs to be built into the culture of an organization. Senior management needs to walk the talk not just issue policy and codes'

'Ethics is essential to a great working environment'

General

'Ethics is a tricky subject as it is intangible and hard to quantify, prove or disprove'

'The over-focus on profits built up in the past 35 years has scuttled much of ethical behaviour'

'There is no such thing as "ethics at work" vs "ethics". It is about how we live and that very separation of work and the rest of our lives is part of the issue'

'In America ethics have to do with saving face, not solving or curtailing injustices or bad behaviours'

'I have heard this expression from my employer "Yes it probably is unethical but it is not illegal"'

'An important issue but our moral values appear to be decreasing'

'Ethical behaviour is basic morality – without it you are no better than low life. You may "improve" the bottom line but at what cost?'

'As a social worker it is something I think about every day. I am sure there are many other areas where it is not really thought about'

NOTES

CHAPTER 2

[1] Careerbuilder.com 2009 survey of 2,700 executives

[2] 'Social networking and reputational risk in the workplace', Deloitte LLP 2009 Ethics & Workplace Survey

CHAPTER 3

[1] Equality and Human Rights Commission 2009. Gender pay activity in large non-public sector organizations

[2] Jim Collins, *Good to Great: Why Some Companies Make the Leap and Others Don't.* Random House Business Books 2001

CHAPTER 4

[1] James O'Toole and Warren Bennis, 'What's Needed Next: A Culture of Candour'. *Harvard Business Review*, June 2009

[2] Ethisphere Institute. World's Most Ethical Companies Ranking

[3] Sally Bibb, 'Ethics in the Workplace' Survey 2010

[4] Joseph Badarracoo, *Leading Quietly: An Unorthodox Guide to Doing the Right Thing.* Harvard Business School Press 2002

CHAPTER 5

[1] Carol Dweck, *Mindset: The new Psychology of Success*. Random House 2006

CHAPTER 6

[1] R. Khurana, *From Higher Aims to Hired Hands*. Princeton University Press 2007
[2] Howard Gardner, 'The Ethical Mind'. *Harvard Business Review* 2007

FURTHER READING

BOOKS

Defining Moments: When Managers Must Choose Between Right and Right. Joseph L. Badaracco. Harvard Business School Press 1997

Why Should Anyone Be Led by You?: What it Takes to be an Authentic Leader. Rob Goffee and Gareth Jones. Harvard Business School Press 2006

Good to Great; Why Some Organisations Make the Leap and Others Don't. Jim Collins. Random House Business Books 2001

Justice: What's the Right Thing to Do. Michael J. Sandel. Allen Lane 2009

Conversations on Ethics. Alex Voorhoeve. Oxford University Press 2009

Giving Voice to Values: How to Speak Your Mind When You Know What's Right. Mary C. Gentile. Yale University Press 2010

A Question of Trust: The Crucial Nature of Trust in Business, Work and Life and How to Build it. Sally Bibb and Jeremy Kourdi. Cyan Books and Marshall Cavendish 2006

The CEO and the Monk. Robert B. Cattell, Kenny Moore, Ken Rifkin. John Wiley and Sons 2004

WEBSITES

www.etisphere.com (articles and World's Most Ethical Company rankings)

www.sallybibb.com (for further articles and discussions on ethics and related issues)

INDEX

Index compiled by Annette Musker